Managing Classroom Behavior and Discipline

Jim Walters, M.A.
and Shelly Frei

Managing Classroom Behavior and Discipline

Editor
Maria Elvira Kessler, M.A.

Project Manager
Maria Elvira Kessler, M.A.

Editor-in-Chief
Sharon Coan, M.S.Ed.

Creative Director
Lee Aucoin

Cover Design
Lesley Palmer

Imaging
Phil Garcia
Don Tran

Publisher
Corinne Burton, M.A.Ed.

Shell Education
5301 Oceanus Drive
Huntington Beach, CA 92649-1030
www.shelleducation.com

ISBN 978-1-4258-0378-0

Table of Contents

Table of Contents *(cont.)*

Table of Contents *(cont.)*

Introduction

The classroom has been called the experimental lab of the child. Because children spend a major part of their formative years in school, it becomes vital to examine the roles of classroom management and discipline as an important dynamic in student experience and success. A controlled classroom environment is essential for effective learning, good teacher-pupil relationships, and peer collaboration. Results of several national Gallup polls clearly document that both the general public and teachers agree that a major problem for public schools is lack of student discipline in classrooms (Elam, Rose, & Gallup, 1996; Rose & Gallup, 2003, 2004).

Schools that typically have a difficult time establishing and enforcing a discipline policy regularly experience teacher burnout and turnover. Many teachers commonly find that approximately one-half of all classroom time can be taken up with activities other than instruction. It can be very difficult for teachers to receive effective training in the right strategies that will allow them more instructional time and less management of behavioral troubles. This is a big problem when considering standards-based educational goals and the rising accountability to meet certain target rates of success for schools, teachers, and students. Conversely, districts that enforce a schoolwide discipline policy help prevent and direct behavior problems by coordinating procedures throughout the school and informing the students extensively of appropriate and inappropriate actions (Gushee, 1984). When teachers do get the right kind of training, real changes can be made in the strategies they use for classroom curriculum instruction and in the organization of basic management approaches. This means more students will be engaged in their learning activities, which will translate to more teaching and learning actually occurring. In fact, discipline is so important that it should be viewed as an extension of the learning process. To facilitate learning, there needs to be order in the classroom. "Order in a classroom simply means that within acceptable limits the students are following the program of action necessary for a particular classroom event to be realized in the situation" (Doyle, 1986, p. 396). To attain this order, teachers must prepare, plan, reflect, and apply effective management strategies, just as they would with every other subject they teach.

The teacher should not stand alone. Key players for establishing and maintaining classroom discipline include the administrators, support staff, parents, every adult who works with the children, and even the students themselves. Effective schoolwide management of children needs to take place on school buses, on the grounds of the school, in the school cafeteria, in the lavatories, in the hallways, and outside the classroom. The administration has an important responsibility to create a positive school climate and culture in order to maintain teacher morale, because the principal controls so many contingencies in the overall work environment (Lumsden, 1998). Yet, the responsibility of classroom discipline ultimately rests with the teacher in each particular classroom.

A classroom with on-task students working toward their learning goals does not happen by accident or luck. Teachers need a deliberate plan to make sure that teaching and learning occur (Allen, 1996). The plan must include activities that engage the students in a variety of ways and hold the students responsible and accountable. Teachers need to plan how they will treat students fairly and with respect. Teachers must make a plan for teaching students to make wise choices and training them that all of their decisions carry consequences. Teachers also need to consider where they might need to make changes to their actual instructional practices in order to prevent behavioral issues that might occur.

Within this book, you will find strategies to help you create order and discipline in your classroom. With this knowledge, you will find a number of application opportunities to practice the content introduced. You will also discover what it takes to set up effective classroom rules. This book will present specific strategies to help you focus energy on the important issues and overlook the nonessential issues that can waste time. The chapters will allow the teacher to critically review current practices and also analyze potential action for actual student behavior issues. Whatever the school population or the present situation, this book will be useful as a tool with practical application questions and activities for your personal development as a classroom teacher.

How This Book Is Organized

The chapters in this book will build on one another and present current research findings. At the end of each chapter there is an opportunity to review and reflect on what you have learned and what it might mean in your own practice. **Chapter 1** asks the pertinent questions, "What is the difference between classroom management and classroom discipline?" and "Is there evidence of either one in my classroom?" The teacher will read about the importance of establishing a positive learning environment in **Chapter 2**. **Chapter 3** discusses practical ways to set up the classroom for success with rules, consequences, signals, and classroom layout. In **Chapter 4**, the teacher will examine tips for engaging students in their learning and keeping them working on task. **Chapter 5** investigates everyday behavior problems that can easily get the teacher off track. **Chapter 6** discusses further strategies for students with elevated behavioral needs. Special considerations for students with special needs will be analyzed in **Chapter 7**. **Chapter 8** helps the teacher understand what parents are going through and how to work with them. The teacher can delve into the benefits of collaboration with colleagues in **Chapter 9**. Finally, **Chapter 10** will help the teacher outline an effective overall classroom management and discipline strategy.

Examine Your Classroom Management Practices

The greatest fear of new teachers across the nation is losing control of a classroom of students. Before starting a new school year, even returning teachers have nightmares about the principal walking into the classroom with the students running around everywhere. These fears are well-founded, because for the majority of educators this is the most difficult aspect of their job. Researchers Dollase (1992) and Gordon (1991) reached this conclusion when they reported that the biggest challenge that teachers face is maintaining discipline and order in their classrooms. When teachers have trouble establishing management and order, their morale takes a beating and they feel that they are not up to the task, resulting in stress and burnout. Teachers who burn out often end up changing their profession. Research in the 1990s showed that over 40 percent of new teachers do not teach longer than four years, and that half of those are actually gone before teaching a full three years (Bernshausen & Cunningham, 2001). More current research from the National Education Association (NEA) shows that this is still true today; they report that 20 percent of all new hires leave within three years. Close to 50 percent of new hires that are placed in urban districts leave the profession before teaching five years (NEA, 2006). Teacher stress commonly affects a teacher's general health and emotional state, as well as the other teachers and the students around them (Wood & McCarthy, 2002).

If this describes you, then take comfort in knowing that you are not alone in respect to your own frustration with class control. One of the primary preventions of teacher burnout is to consult with other educators on issues that directly impact their classrooms (Wood & McCarthy, 2002). This book will explore the vital concerns surrounding classroom discipline and management. Harry and Rosemary Wong, whose book *The First Days of School* (1998) is often given to new teachers, write, "Student achievement at the end of the year is directly related to the degree to which the teacher establishes good control of the classroom procedures in the very first week of the school year" (p. 4).

The correlation between management and student success should provide teachers with the motivation to examine their practices from the beginning of the school year. This book contains multiple levels of application and reflection. The goal for this reflection is to identify the need for the most effective strategies that will result in reaching high student achievement. The end of each chapter, as well as application activities throughout the chapters, will allow you to reflect on your current practices in the specific topical areas. The final chapter will offer the opportunity to plan for a successful future involving classroom discipline.

Classroom Management vs. Classroom Discipline

Before continuing, it is important to draw attention to the difference between the terms *classroom management* and *classroom discipline.* Although they are often used interchangeably, they are actually two different topics. Classroom management refers to how things are generally carried out in the classroom, whereas classroom discipline is the specific management of student behavior. Dr. Marvin Marshall explains, "Classroom management deals with how things are done; discipline deals with how people behave. Classroom management has to do with procedures, routines, and structure; discipline is about impulse management and self-control. Classroom management is the teacher's responsibility; discipline is the student's responsibility" (Marshall, 2003, para. 7).

The reason these terms are often used synonymously is that the teacher first has to set up how the classroom functions in order to expect the students to behave. Simply put, effective teachers *manage* their classrooms with procedures and routines. This process often takes care of many of the concerns surrounding classroom discipline. In contrast, ineffective teachers only attempt to *discipline* their students with threats and punishments rather than laying a foundation with effective procedures for the learning environment (Wong & Wong, 1998). It is no wonder that the most significant issue on the minds of most new teachers is that of controlling their students. Inexperienced teachers often do not have the time to develop successful strategies and thus burn out early in their careers (Bernshausen & Cunningham, 2001). Classroom management includes the organization of students, space, time, and materials so that the teacher can then allow the students to learn the intended content (Wong & Wong, 1998). It remains a challenge for veteran teachers as well, as each year brings a fresh group of students for whom to establish management practices.

Of all the things teachers are expected to do during their professional days, classroom discipline is perhaps the most significant and is clearly of concern to many parents and teachers alike (Langdon, 1996). When considering classroom discipline, it is first important to consider that without order provided by effective classroom management, there is little hope for teachers to instruct in any consistent and effective manner. When teachers feel that they need to discipline students, it is often because there was a lack of procedures and routine in place (Wong & Wong, 1998). Classroom learning requires classroom order and, while it may be very difficult, it is central to what educators need to do.

Additionally, classroom discipline is absolutely necessary for instilling a sense of responsibility and maturity in the students. Each time a teacher works with children in an effort to modify their behavior, both parties should be able to observe and better understand what is being expected of them.

Examine Your Current Practices

With that in mind, the self-assessments on pages 16 and 17 will allow you to scrutinize your own practices in your classroom. In order to obtain an accurate view of your own current teaching practices, you shouldn't try to second guess your initial response. An accurate score will come from what you think actually describes your teaching practice and not what you wish your teacher practices would be on a day-to-day basis. Only by honestly reflecting on existing practices and challenges can you begin to see what needs to change and how you can embark on making valuable modifications. These reflection tools are not meant to be used in an administrative evaluation context for any teacher. They are simply provided for teachers to honestly reveal to themselves where they are weakest so that they will know where to focus their energy on strengthening their classroom management practices. The first assessment, "Rate Your Role in the Classroom Environment," will allow you to rate your overall role in facilitating a well-managed classroom. The second assessment, "Rate Your Teaching Responses," will allow you to examine your general response to students and situations.

Rate Your Role in the Classroom Environment

Rate yourself within your current classroom by reading the statements below and labeling them with a Y (Yes) or an N (No).

_____ I understand the different types of students I have and I take this into consideration when planning a lesson, an activity, or a field trip.

_____ I clearly communicate my classroom management expectations to my students.

_____ I follow through with consequences when classroom rules are broken.

_____ My students know what to do when they finish an assignment.

_____ My discipline is somewhat flexible according to the student.

_____ I don't typically lose instructional time due to discipline problems.

_____ I usually understand why a child is acting out or not doing his/her best.

_____ I always address student problems in an appropriate and timely manner.

_____ I use a variety of intervention methods.

_____ I teach my students how to solve their problems independently.

_____ My students are encouraged to work out their interpersonal problems without teacher help.

_____ My students help other students deal with problems.

_____ My students want to be in my class.

_____ My students feel safe in my class.

_____ I follow a systematic approach to classroom management.

_____ I have a signal to get my students' immediate attention.

How many **Yes** answers do you have in the survey above? __________

Out of the total 16 responses, what is your percentage of maintaining a successful classroom environment? __________

$$\frac{\text{\# of Yes answers}}{16} = \frac{\text{Your percentage (\%)}}{100\%}$$

Rate Your Teaching Responses

For each of the following areas, circle the number on each scale that most accurately matches your response.

1. **My requests to students are**

   1 2 3 4 5 6 7 8 9 10
   Ambiguous — Clear

2. **My requests to the students are phrased**

   1 2 3 4 5 6 7 8 9 10
   Negatively — Positively

3. **When I want student compliance, I usually use**

   1 2 3 4 5 6 7 8 9 10
   Questions — Direct Requests

4. **When I make a request, I usually use a**

   1 2 3 4 5 6 7 8 9 10
   Loud voice — Quiet voice

5. **My state of mind when I respond to student behavior is**

   1 2 3 4 5 6 7 8 9 10
   Emotional — Calm

6. **After a request I usually**

   1 2 3 4 5 6 7 8 9 10
   Immediately go on to something else — Watch for compliance

7. **I require compliance in (mark the number of seconds)**

   1 2 3 4 5 6 7 8 9 10

You can add up the points for each response above:

63–70: You seem to have *an exceptional ability* to respond to the varying conditions of daily classroom situations.

56–62: Your score indicates *very good teacher responses* as you meet the challenges involved in each day.

49–55: You have shown *a fair ability* to calmly address classroom issues.

42–48: Your score highlights the areas in which you might *need improvement.*

1–41: Your total shows that there are various areas in which you might *need guidance and coaching* in order to establish a positive environment of classroom management.

Taking the Time to Reflect

The next step to classroom management is to examine the information you have just gathered when rating your management practices. Attention will be given throughout this book to the importance of teacher reflection toward continuous improvement. In order to become successful, teachers need time to think about practices and then share concerns and questions frequently with teachers they deem successful and credible in order to gain new insight and ideas (Bernshausen & Cunningham, 2001). Certainly, there is a significant amount of thinking about what occurs in the classroom, but most of it falls very short of effective reflection that leads to authentic positive transformation. If a teacher never questions the goals and the values that guide his/her work, the context in which he/she teaches, or his/her assumptions, then this type of "reflection" will be shallow and fruitless.

This process, painful as it may be, is pivotal and beneficial for teachers in training, as well as for new and veteran teachers (Ferraro, 2000). Critical reflection is an important aspect of both teaching and learning. Teachers learn from those experiences that they contemplate, explore, review, and question. Teachers don't learn from experience alone; it takes reflection. From this critical process, teachers can begin to recognize differences from their own practices and those of successful practitioners; this is commonly viewed as an efficient technique for professional development and an effective way to more efficiently influence student academic success (Ferraro, 2000). Each teacher needs to decide what is reasonable and helpful while planning future experiences. It's only through reflection that one can gauge actions in order to further the goal of being a more professional educator. Teachers need to develop a thoughtful problem-solving disposition toward teaching.

After you have taken the self-assessments on pages 16 and 17, you may be doubting your choice of vocation. Perhaps now you are even thinking that you do not have the right personality for teaching. This is natural and can actually be quite healthy, if appropriate actions are then taken. Low assessment scores do not mean that you are not fit for the profession; it simply means you are probably working twice as hard but only getting half the results.

Left unchallenged, feelings of self-doubt or excuses can prevent you from acting on your most creative ideas. After looking at your scores on the self-assessments, you may feel disappointed. Again, this is normal. Keep in mind that the process of reflection will become easier and more meaningful the more it is practiced. Start by reading through the chapters in this book and reflecting on each aspect of classroom management that is discussed. Take the time to fill in the idea boxes provided throughout the chapters and then complete the reflection questions at the end of each chapter.

Reflection helps you to learn who you are as a teacher and to be aware of how you teach. Your work is complex and requires constant and deep reflection, so do not try to hurry through the process. Over time, this can significantly affect and direct your professional choices and decisions. Getting that great blend of classroom management with a positive atmosphere should not be a mystery.

Establishing Strategies That Inspire Student Academic Success

All teachers, of course, have different personalities, but they also have a lot in common, including the fact that many of them entered the profession in order to help students learn. They are often included in the professional category with others in serving industries, such as those who become nurses, counselors, ministers, and social workers. Writers Harry and Rosemary Wong go further, saying "Teachers are in the helping and caring profession, a service profession to help people enhance the quality of their lives" (1998, p. 21). With a responsibility as great as this, teachers often feel an insatiable need to help others and finish the day with positive expectations for student behavior and achievement. Optimistic teachers believe that they can influence student learning and positively affect their lives. It is vital that teachers demonstrate positive expectations toward all students, because research shows that whatever the teacher expects is generally what the learner tends to produce (Wong & Wong, 1998). Teachers go into the teaching profession with the best of intentions but will still be ineffective without productive classroom management strategies.

In order to establish dynamic strategies in the area of classroom management, you have to be in charge of your students, the space around them, the time allotted for your content area or areas and how you use it, and the materials needed so that everyone in your class is effectively learning. There definitely is a link between how well-managed your classroom is and how much your students achieve (Marzano, Marzano, & Pickering, 2003). Through all your efforts, you are essentially trying to do two things: enhance student involvement and cooperation and establish a positive working environment.

Every educator has a different idea of what makes a good teacher. In all areas, including discipline, teachers glean ideas from their own personal experiences while growing up, past teaching experiences, and the advice and ideas from other educators. Sometimes it is difficult to go off of personal memory or even the advice of another teacher because it is difficult to second-guess what some other person might do in a given situation. You might think that a particular method, style, or point of view is the best way to do something and then end up frustrated when it doesn't fit your teaching style or work for a particularly challenging group of students. Try to be someone else and you will almost always get poor results. There is definitely room for individualism and flexibility in the profession of teaching. Teachers need to reflect and then act upon strategies that will work with their personal styles and the needs of their particular students. It is a continuous, changing process as new students come into your classroom and your teaching approaches evolve.

Teacher Conduct

Before we examine the behavior of the students, it is very important to examine the general conduct of the teacher. The teacher's attitude, educational pedagogy, planning, preparation, and conduct are going to affect how students respond in the classroom. It is essential that students perceive teachers as confident, in charge, and fair. For this to happen, the teacher must establish himself/herself as an appropriate authority figure and role model. Often when students are challenging a teacher's authority, the teacher may unwittingly follow with a counterproductive negative emotional response. However, there are several key components that need to be in place in order to avoid any such situation. By carefully planning lessons, knowing the students, having a discipline action plan, and learning from past mistakes, teachers can avoid their own exaggerated emotional responses to disrespectful students, as well as avoiding subsequent defiant outbursts from the students (Fischer, 2004). While teachers are expected to be caring, dedicated, skillful, sensitive, flexible, and responsive, most of all they must be the authority figure in the classroom.

One of the top mistakes of new teachers is to try to be too friendly with students. While a friendly rapport with students is certainly desired and might come later in the year, the beginning of the year is the time to establish rules, expectations, and order. The teacher can still develop a friendly rapport by personally greeting each student upon entering the classroom and then starting the day officially with the expectation of correct behavior and high standards for learning. Some teachers will have their students show signals as they enter the room to show how they are feeling. For example, a student who shows the number one is having a bad morning and the student showing a five feels great. As you go through your own learning process about which strategies work best for you, be patient with your own learning curve and with your students (Starr, 2005).

Respecting Students

Fundamental to any workable program is respect for your students. It is important to accept the students you have, not the students you wish you had. To elevate yourself to this level, you will first have to think of each individual student as a person who deserves to be treated with dignity, regardless of his/her intellectual abilities, primary language, social training, cultural background, or personal circumstance. Those who have been treated unfairly may become scapegoats or targets of violence by their peers. If teachers treat students fairly, they are more likely to respect one another. In some cases, students may react in aggressive ways. Some children have been constantly disrespected even by their own family members for years. Here, it is vital that the teacher persevere in showing them that they not only deserve respect but can live up to that respect.

Effective schools communicate with a deliberate and systematic effort to students and the greater community that all children are valued and respected; for example, displaying children's artwork, posting academic work prominently throughout the classroom, respecting students' diversity (Dwyer, Osther, & Warger, 1999). Students respond to adults who respect them and hold them to high expectations of successful learning. At the start of each school day, teacher Jennifer Moorhouse, who has taught in Illinois, Texas, and California, writes the day's objectives on the board along with the question "What do we need to do today to be successful in today's lessons?" The class makes a plan and she moves into the day's lessons. She reinforces the plan with a message such as "You are accountable for your learning by accomplishing these tasks." Tell students again and again that they are important and that you require them to live up to that standard. This produces a more confident student and proportionally reduces your discipline problems.

Dignifying Students

At first glance, dignifying students seems to be the same thing as respecting them, but it actually takes it one step further. You dignify others when you demonstrate interest in their lives, ideas, and activities. On the schoolwide level, schools that accomplish this are the ones where parents feel invited to participate and to be present on campus. These schools celebrate and validate the various cultures and languages represented in a school. By dignifying students' efforts, teachers in the classroom create an atmosphere where students feel welcomed, valued, and respected. Glasser (2000) even went so far as to suggest that teachers adopt seven connecting habits—caring, listening, supporting, contributing, encouraging, trusting, and befriending.

The teacher's goal should be to interface with students as an extension of his/her own authority rather than simply attempting to control. Students will normally accept fair and reasonable rules and consequences when they know that you are genuinely concerned about their well-being. This means that they should not be singled out or used as negative examples. When you have had to repeatedly or strongly correct a student, it is important that before the student leaves for the day you reconnect and show that you care about, believe in, and sincerely want what is best for him/her. Perhaps you will want to take this child aside and explain that he/she is a role model for some of the others. With this kind of positive responsibility, they will generally live up to your expectations. The key is to continually validate the student. "You are important." "I know you can be one of the best . . . ." "Others are depending on you to . . . ." "I'm on your side." These types of statements not only redirect the students from counterproductive behavior, but they also provide them with hope.

Keeping Control of Your Emotions

It is extremely important for you to control your emotions and not lose your temper. This sort of immediate reaction usually reflects a teacher's own lack of confidence in dealing with a given situation (Fischer, 2004). As the adult, you should model appropriate behavior even under highly stressful situations. If you lose self-control, it becomes more difficult for you to make the proper decisions under the circumstances and also to retain the respect of your students (Fischer, 2004). When you lose your cool, behavior becomes the focus of attention rather than the students and their learning. If you feel yourself getting too agitated, take a deep breath and examine what is going on for five seconds. If necessary, assign a few minutes of individual work and take some time to sift through papers at your desk. Then, move in to control the situation, and as you walk, place your hands behind your back. This is less threatening to the students and may possibly save you from inappropriately using your hands.

Maintaining a Calm Voice

Using different vocal inflections in the classroom is appropriate only if it has a legitimate educational purpose, does not demean students, and does not result in yelling, which is ineffective and abusive. Some teachers use loud projecting voices and find that they have to keep getting louder in order to compete with the 30 other voices in their rooms. These teachers might find themselves without a voice at all, or a very hoarse one. Other teachers resort to fear tactics, such as yelling at students. Authors Nelson, Lott, and Glenn's case study (2000) showed an example of a teacher who was openly hostile with her students. Whenever students misbehaved, she yelled at them, criticized them, and humiliated them in front of their classmates. Using fear tactics to gain control does not prove conducive to learning. Students generally shut down completely or amp up and yell back in these situations. You will generally have much more control, as well as credibility, with your students, their parents, and your superiors if you never raise your voice (Fischer, 2004).

One of the most valuable voice techniques teachers can use is a stage whisper, because it is human nature for children to want to know what is being whispered. The teacher should get as close to them as possible and whisper as loudly as possible until they are straining to hear. Since it is impossible for every student to hear you the first time, do not expect them to calm down the moment you start. Give them a few seconds and watch what happens.

Eye Contact

Direct eye contact and nonverbal communication are effective classroom management tools, provided that they don't become inappropriate or intimidating to students. When a student is misbehaving or breaking a class rule, simply pause and look him/her in the eye. This is not to be intended as a threatening gesture, but one of authority. Many times, you won't even need to say a thing—the student will feel the power of your stare. Eye contact is also used as a preventative measure for discipline problems. Your students want some signal from you that validates their presence in the class. Get in the habit of scanning the room once every few minutes to know what is going on and to let the students know you value them being a part of the group. It is also very important to be aware of the cultural norms represented in your classroom. Students in some cultures are trained that eye contact from a student to an authority figure is rude. Thus, do not necessarily demand it of students, "Look at me when I speak to you," because they might be demonstrating respect by looking down.

Praise and Correction

Teachers like to be complimented and validated, and students aren't any different. Students crave attention. Sometimes, a student is so deprived of attention that he/she will invite even negative attention through rude behavior. Therefore, public praise in the classroom can be a very powerful tool. This can be a quick strategy that involves subtly recognizing a student with a positive gesture. When it comes to correction, it is generally more powerful and appropriate to correct students individually and privately. This applies to students at every grade level. However, it might also be appropriate to direct positive correction in the form of an affirmation, such as "Pay attention, you are very important to us." Students who are corrected in front of their peers often respond by acting out even more, because they are responding to that unconscious or conscious need for attention. It is ineffective to engage in disciplinary conversation from across the room (Starr, 2005). A general guideline level is to correct privately and to praise publicly.

One way to publicly praise students is to have an impromptu praise time when you go around the room and say one or two sentences about as many children as you can. Many, but not all, students love being singled out if there are others getting the same degree of attention. Compliments should always be genuine, specific, and never contrived. It is up to the teacher to ensure that they are evenly distributing praise, if done publicly. Remember that your students use you as a gauge to see how they are doing. If you like what you see, let them know immediately.

Again, it is very important to be aware of the cultural norms represented in the classroom. There are certain cultural and religious groups in which being in the spotlight is uncomfortable, no matter if the situation is negative or positive. Furthermore, some experts have found praise to be counterproductive in that it can cause students to lose any confidence to give an answer without the teacher's evaluation immediately expressed. Additionally, not all students seek to please the teacher, especially as they grow older (Hitz & Driscoll, 1989). Teachers can evaluate their use of praise by videotaping a typical lesson and then judging the motivation for praise used and how it seemed to affect the various children in the classroom. Praising should encourage self-confidence and autonomy in the willingness to take risks in learning.

Encouragement

One step further is to give encouragement. With reassurance, you may no longer need to use prizes or rewards. Reassurance shows children unconditional love and acceptance and separates them from their actions. With this support, they see that mistakes can become opportunities for learning. You become inspiring and stimulating without appearing to be judgmental or manipulating. This does not mean you have to "dummy down" your course or give false support, but it does mean you can build scaffolds, academically and emotionally. It also entails providing prompt and detailed qualitative feedback on how well your student is doing. "The students will catch the spirit and will probably come up with other ways to practice encouragement in the classroom" (Nelsen, Lott, & Glenn, 2000, p. 164). Hitz and Driscoll (1989) recommend that, rather than using praise, teachers encourage their students. According to them, encouragement differs from praise, as teachers offer specific honest and private feedback on improvement and effort, rather than using evaluative words publicly in order to manage and manipulate the work of all the children in the classroom.

Teacher Jennifer Moorhouse sets up two charts for her middle school seventh-graders at the beginning of the year. On the inside portion of the student chart, she writes a general goal that will be hard for them to attain, such as an "A" grade on the upcoming quarterly math assessments. Then, on the teacher chart, she writes a personal goal of hers that is hard for her to attain, such as running to stay in shape. On the inside of each graphic organizer, she writes down what needs to occur in order for those goals to be reached. On the outside, she writes down what prevents both her and the students from accomplishing the goals. Then, she connects the goals by adding that if the students work toward their hard goals, she will work toward her hard goal; namely, for each "A" on the next quarterly exam, she will run a lap around the track. Now she has students motivated to work hard as they relate attaining their goal to their own teacher's motivations for working hard in life toward goals as well. This encouraging environment can ultimately simplify the job of teaching as students are motivated to be engaged in their learning processes.

Listen Before You Discipline

It is important to listen carefully to students and to consider their points of view before disciplinary action is taken. Listening to students is particularly important when there is a situation in which you may not have all the pertinent or correct information. When you can take the time to do this, you demonstrate a sincere respect for the child's sense of self worth. Teacher knowledge of student thinking is critical. Gathercoal (2001) has written that teachers need to listen and hear what students are saying as they conjecture and build arguments. Only then can they judge the quality of students' justifications and explanations.

The process of listening will not only assist you in making proper decisions, but also will often result in a teachable moment for everyone involved. Sometimes, the greater issue isn't the problem at hand. Keep an open mind for an underlying situation or frustration that may need to be addressed. If an incident occurs in class and you don't have time to get into a discussion, you can say something like, "I'd like you to work over there by yourself so that no one bothers you." This way, you have given the redirection immediately and done it in a positive manner. Some teachers keep a notebook in the back of the classroom in which students are invited to write issues that arise in the classroom. The teacher reads the notebook at the end of each day and can be aware of ongoing problems between students and address concerns when necessary.

Giving Directions

Even the seemingly simple process of expressing directions can be stated in an affirming way. Examples include, "We need you to pay attention so that you don't miss vital information," or "You are important to this discussion." Other times, you need to give specific expectations in your directions. When you are confronted with a student who needs constant redirection, you might need to take these further steps: look the student in the eye, call him/her by name, use close proximity, and use appropriate verbal and non-verbal cues. The use of a student's name pronounced correctly automatically conveys to that student that he/she is important to you (Wong & Wong, 1998). Consider specific goal-directed messages such as: "Mary, sit down in your chair now; work quietly, finish these ten problems, and do not get up until the bell rings." "John, stop hitting Sue now, and do not hit anyone else ever again in this class." Give the student sufficient time to process the direction, decide to comply, and then actually obey after giving a request. During this waiting interval, do not converse or argue; rather, look the student in the eye, restate the request if required, and wait for compliance. All of this is to be done in a calm and even tone of voice.

Avoiding Confrontations With Students

Arguments are merely power struggles. As the teacher, you already are the authority, so you have no need to argue. Never get into an argument with students regardless of what they may say. These confrontations are pointless, they are futile, and they make you appear unprofessional. Students who disagree with what the teacher requires should be encouraged to discuss those concerns privately. They should not be allowed to argue with the teacher in front of other students or to publicly challenge the teacher's authority. If a student continues to press the point after you have told him/her what to do, simply say, "Nevertheless . . . ." and restate your point.

Eliminate the Use of Threats

One of the reasons that children can behave perfectly without any problems for some teachers, but are uncontrollable with others, is the issue of conducting oneself in a respectful manner. Teachers must use their superior positions and confidence to gain compliance. You should never threaten students. While threatening might cause temporary compliance, the strategy will not help children make ethical, wise decisions about behavior in the future (Kohn, 1994). Allowing yourself to get carried away with such strong emotional reactions will always be counterproductive, and you will probably regret it later (Fischer, 2004). Rather, be consistent and do not forewarn consequences that you are unable or unwilling to deliver.

Clearly spell out the cost of students' choices and then be prepared to back up your words by consistently enforcing the rules. It is much better to say nothing than risk saying something that cannot be followed through. This is a great example of the necessity of clear expectations from the onset of the school year. If there is a readily seen and accepted list of rules and consequences, then the teacher does not constantly have to come up with consequences to enforce. The students will not be surprised when consequences are enforced. Even if they choose to make the same choice every day with a negative behavior, there will be consistency in the consequence that they are then choosing.

Chapter 1 Reflection

1. What do you consider to be your underlying philosophy or values for creating and maintaining a controlled classroom environment?

2. How does this chapter discussion change your view of your own teaching practices as they pertain to classroom management and discipline?

3. Now that you have explored the difference between classroom management and classroom discipline, write down two strengths and two weaknesses that you have in the area of established classroom management as it pertains to student behavior that is exhibited in your classroom.

Providing a Positive Learning Environment

Classroom environments have climates as do regions and locations. You instinctively know there are places in which you would not like to live. Your impression can extend beyond just the physical aspects of the common weather patterns and how a place looks—although those things are certainly important. Additionally, a place can affect your ability to feel relaxed or comfortable. You often sense whether you will like a place as you observe the way people interact with one another, how they listen, and what they say. This variation of physical and emotional ambience is found in classrooms as well. The classroom is often a direct reflection of the teacher who has physically set it up and expressively established the ambience of it. The teacher's attitudes, emotions, and educational pedagogy affect the way he/she physically arranges the room, and these things also affect how the teacher establishes the classroom procedures and routines. This in turn affects how students, parents, and others feel as they walk into a classroom.

The Emotional and Physical Environments

One of the most important aspects a teacher can foster for a positive classroom environment is the overall attitude. Remember that even an unmovable bureaucracy, an unsupportive parent, or a belligerent student does not have to affect your feelings or make you angry unless you allow them to. You owe it to your students and yourself to remain calm and in charge of your emotions. It is possible and very important for you to maintain a collegial, enthusiastic, and positive learning environment. Marzano recommends that you honestly reflect on your own bias toward difficult students by mentally reviewing each student, anticipating problems, and visualizing successful outcomes with each student (Marzano, Marzano, & Pickering, 2003). Your effort will have great benefits; if you give your students a more positive attitude and higher expectations, they will be able to give you back more than you expected from them (Wong & Wong, 1998). This produces a much lower level of personal stress and, at the end of the day, you are happier and more productive. It makes sense to learn how to meet the common frustrations and disappointments that can be commonly met in a classroom in a constructive way.

Everyone likes to end the day feeling good about themselves and their work environments, but few jobs allow you to create a physical atmosphere to fit your personality. Teaching definitely qualifies as one of those positions. Teachers can usually choose the colors displayed, the words posted, the amount of clutter that might contribute to student distractions, the visuals, the type of student work shown, and the amount of used wall space. Teachers can choose to post motivational phrases, inspirational photographs, and encouraging displays of student academic progress. Teachers choose the formation of the desks, which directly affects the types of activities allowed in the classroom.

Connecting the Constructed Environment to Instructional Lessons

In both the physical and emotional realms, the most important goal is to direct and inspire student learning. Any teacher desiring a positive learning environment should begin with the suggestions on pages 36 and 37. These suggestions will take the teacher through the process of considering physical setup of a classroom (which will be discussed further in Chapter 3), emotional responses to students in the classroom and, most importantly, well-planned instructional lessons that move students through the learning process.

Through adjustments in teaching practices, effective teachers can literally invite students to join the learning process involved in everyday lessons (Wong & Wong, 1998). Such adjustments include consideration of the affective environment when students enter and spend the day or period in the classroom; the physical setup that determines how students move through the room with materials and during activities; the overall management system that facilitates student knowledge of rules, expectations, and consequences; and, most importantly, well-planned instructional time that allows students to learn the necessary curriculum topics.

- Think about how your individual students best learn. Remember past lessons that have worked well and why they did. Set up your classroom in a way that will facilitate the types of activities that are most motivating for student progress.
- Use more than one strategy when teaching each lesson. Ideally, you will be giving your class a lesson in which they hear, see, and manipulate to better understand what you want them to learn. Create physical space for the movement, from direct classroom lecturing, to group-oriented cooperative or centers activities, to room for quiet independent work.
- Remember to address the particular needs of students who have special needs or IEPs. (This will be addressed specifically in Chapter 7.)
- Prepare your students to make smooth transitions and rehearse transitions so they are all under 30 seconds. At the beginning of the year and after a big break, the students will need ample opportunities to practice.
- Establish and practice your signals. Students need practice responding to your signals during independent work, group work, and whole-class activities.
- Conduct lessons at a brisk pace and provide continuous tasks on which students can focus. Reflect on unnecessary time, such as preparation for the end of a class period or recess time. Often, students are given too much time and then problems can occur.
- Check constantly for student understanding. Plan for the ways in which the lesson can be adjusted as the needs of the students change.

- Vary the types and levels of questions you use. It's a great idea to plan various questions at different levels of thinking. Consider skill ability and, if necessary, levels of language acquisition if you have English language learners in your class. Have a plan, such as color-coded popsicle sticks that help you quickly direct the right kind of question toward the proper level of student.
- Keep your students actively involved. There should be plenty of time for students to participate in all four domains—reading activities, writing activities, speaking activities, and listening activities—throughout your planned lessons.

Next, anticipate that things will not always go the way you want. How will you handle the student who is argumentative, inattentive, or manipulative? If you raise your voice regularly, stoop to negativity, or lose control, you will no longer be in charge. Play a game with yourself in which you try to put a positive spin on everything that happens around you. If one of your students isn't paying attention, you should make motivating statements, such as, "You are important to this class, and when you don't pay attention, the class loses out." If he/she wants to argue, you should plan to refute the attempt by saying, "I don't argue with students, sorry." When you meet with someone else who wants to be in charge you can say, "No thank you. I'll handle that." The key is to stay firm, yet positive. You want to maintain an authoritative tone without being condemning.

How to Help Children Feel Good About Themselves

A classroom with a positive learning environment will hopefully include children who feel confident about their abilities and efforts in their learning journeys. In order for people to perceive themselves as able to cope with life's changing demands and to achieve what they need and want to in life, they need to develop the sense that they can reach their personal goals (Walz, 1991). This process strongly relates to the development of a child's self-esteem. Children often judge themselves by the way they think the important people in their lives feel about them. Many times, these "important people" are the peers around them. This becomes increasingly true as students grow older. These peers are also caught up in their own processes of identifying themselves, making them less willing to build up the self-esteem of others around them. Therefore, parents and teachers must do all they can to help children feel that they are unique and special. Teachers spend a very large portion of the day with students, making them significant people in their lives. When important people intentionally use kind words and actions, they increase the probability of receiving positive behaviors in return (Wong & Wong, 1998).

It is imperative that teachers start the school year by treating everyone inside and outside of the classroom with equal respect. Self-esteem will be most evident in classrooms where students receive the right kind of positive meaningful feedback in the form of appreciation, not empty praise (Katz, 1993). The teacher gives clear expectations that the same behavior is expected from all the students. This quickly becomes a two-way street. If you are negative and belittle your students, then they will learn to act the same way toward other students and you. If, on the other hand, you constantly tell students that they are important, they will eventually believe this and behave accordingly. Some students have a hard time showing respect to others because it has not been modeled appropriately or unconditionally to them.

One of the best ways to help a child develop healthy self-esteem is to find and emphasize his/her strengths. This process requires moving beyond activities that merely encourage narcissism, e.g., students simply listing positive things about themselves, into activities that provide curiosity to genuinely explore themselves and others around them (Katz, 1993). Students generally don't need to hear about their weaknesses, as they are normally already aware of them, but teachers can encourage exploration into how they can further effectively strengthen weak areas. Students should have the chance to utilize and apply criteria for evaluating their own work, thus strengthening their own self-esteem (Katz, 1993).

The issue of self-esteem can be even more complicated for students in the classroom who are English language learners. These students are struggling with learning English, learning the academic content, and sometimes dealing with a large mismatch of the culture they are learning and the culture they return home to each night. Because of the cultural mismatch, their parents may not understand the procedures and activities at school either. These are added pressures on these students. The school and the teacher can considerably help these students. The extent to which each language and culture is validated, encouraged, and celebrated is significantly related to how well students achieve academic success, as well as self-esteem and pride in their linguistic and other talents (Cummins, 1991). The teacher can encourage the students to share their language usage, provide opportunities for their languages to be an asset in the classroom, and incorporate multilingual and multicultural displays and resource materials while content is being taught. By translating any letters or handouts sent home, the teacher also validates the students' need for parental involvement in students' academic journeys.

Teachers should encourage children in areas of both strengths and weaknesses and find ways to recognize each child as special. They should avoid the natural tendency to compare one child with another. In order to encourage the students, teachers often have to stop and listen. As a teacher, practice active listening, in which you repeat what students have said to you and then speculate and recap how certain situations might make them feel. This will help you to better understand their points of view. When you have the time, invite students to express all their feelings appropriately.

There will be many times when you have to redirect your students. It is important to separate the incorrect behaviors that lead to mistakes from a student's actual identity of being a good or bad person. Use words that redirect the student's behavior, not words that evaluate his/her actual identity. A child's natural tendency will be to internalize any criticism. It is very important to give children tools that they can use to avoid making the same mistakes in the future. Teach them to discover acceptable ways to behave in areas where they are having difficulty. In these ways, educators can emphasize to students the expectation that they are people who can manage life's realities and demands and that they are worthy of happiness (Walz, 1991).

During the first week of school, have everyone write one unique thing about themselves on a piece of paper. It can be an exciting place they have visited, a special accomplishment, an activity they enjoy doing, or anything that is unique about themselves. When each student has one thing written, have the class stand in a circle. The teacher introduces the activity by announcing that the class will celebrate uniqueness and find commonalities all at the same time. Each student gets to read his/her statement. Then, anyone who has any connection at all to that statement can step into the circle and share their commonality. While this takes some time, there is great value in allowing students to honor their individuality and even greater value in allowing the class to recognize the many ways in which they are similar to one another. An activity such as this allows children to collect information about the whole class. The process validates what is unique about them and, more importantly, how their uniqueness actually connects them to fit in with a group of peers.

Consider the Affective Filter

As every teacher knows, students often enter a classroom with a multitude of problems that can get in the way of learning. Sometimes, they have already been criticized that day by parents, other teachers, friends, or other students. They may also be experiencing anxiety about something going on at home, a situation with the peer group, a future test in another class, or other concerns. English language learners or students with special needs enter your classroom with even more concerns as they prepare to try to understand the day's lessons and the fear of being misunderstood, becoming frustrated, or keeping up with the pace and materials of the class. All of these issues can cause the student's affective filter, which is best envisioned as an invisible screen that rises when stressful or emotional situations occur, to come up so that all learning will be blocked for that time period.

Some teachers continue using more aggressive teaching practices, such as calling on a student and then asking a question. The reason this can raise an affective filter is that the student gets nervous about being able to answer a question before he/she even hears what it is. Lack of sufficient wait time or lack of time to process and practice rehearsing learned information with peers can also cause the affective filter to rise. The term is often applied to English language learners, and it was made famous by Stephen Krashen (1982). He links it to anxiety, motivation, and self-confidence. In actuality, the concept can be useful for all teachers to consider for all students. Every successful teacher should consider nonthreatening and encouraging ways to lower a student's affective filter in order to promote learning. This can be done in a multitude of ways.

The teacher should plan strategies that do not result in anxiety. Rather than the typical practice of calling a name, asking a question, and expecting the answer, a few more successful strategies when asking questions are: allow sufficient think time; allocate time for sorting notes or cards related to the questions beforehand; or permit partners to think of the answer together before calling on students to answer the questions. Teachers lower the affective filter when they plan various activities to help the students dissect difficult material in the textbook. Teachers should offer procedures for students to seek help during activities. When the learning environment is structured, instruction is scaffolded, and there are opportunities for students to experience success, then student frustration can be alleviated (Echevarria, Vogt, & Short, 2004). These are all ways that teachers can lower the affective filter and increase a student's ability to learn the planned content for that day.

What Are Your Expectations?

Before you can create a positive experience in your classroom, you must plan how you will provide clear expectations for your students. It is important to continually restate expectations in an ongoing basis. When telling students what is desired, positive statements have a more powerful influence than negative ones. Many students respond more readily to "Please walk" instead of "Don't run." This concept extends to the overall messages that teachers send about the learning process. For example, tell students "You can successfully study for this upcoming exam" instead of "Don't waste your study time" or "You'll never pass this test if you don't study!" Also, allowing students to share in the decision-making process behind classroom processes can allow them to feel positive about expressing their voices as they help in the direction of their learning processes (Kordalewski, 1999). Expectations should be expressed clearly to students about the classroom procedures, the day's lesson's task activities, the lesson-learning objectives and goals, and the expected outcomes from each day's lessons.

Role play is a powerful way to demonstrate expected behaviors for lesson activities and learning goals. Once you have had some fun acting out a skill, practice it repeatedly. Rather than being wasted time, consider it an investment for the rest of the school year. You will get student buy-in if they think of it as a game rather than a chore. When planning for a lesson activity, sometimes a "fish bowl" process can be effective, wherein a small group of students volunteer to practice in front of the whole group, and then the class discusses which actions were appropriate and which actions could have been improved. As the teacher strives for a positive learning environment and teaches the rules and procedures that will facilitate that in daily instructional activities, he/she also needs to decide beforehand which behavioral issues will be dealt with immediately and which are minor and can be ignored, or at least delayed during instructional time.

Establishing a positive learning environment includes an entire spectrum of teacher actions and expectations. A teacher's smile and the way the teacher greets students entering the classroom can guide students toward the academic means desired, just as the actual setup of the classroom and a well-planned lesson can facilitate a student's ability to learn the day's lesson objectives. Table 2.1 demonstrates some alternative actions for creating a positive learning environment. They are positive approaches for encouraging and motivating students toward success in their content learning. Teachers can look at each tip and reflect on how their classrooms rate.

Table 2.1: Alternative Ways to Help Provide a Positive Learning Environment

Instead of . . .	Try . . .
marking –4 to indicate four mistakes on a test	marking +6 to indicate the number of correct answers.
praising an individual student out loud	praising the pupil privately and praising the class publicly.
putting names of misbehaving students on the board	putting names of achievers, good citizens, etc., on the board or special chart.
repeatedly explaining the directions	modeling the response desired with a few practice examples.
nagging the child who is not working	saying "I am so happy with those of you who are working well."
criticizing the class for poor test performance	praising the class for what they did correctly. After reinstruction, ask them to see if they can improve their scores the second time around.
talking at length with a child after his/her misbehavior	simply telling him/her you were disappointed in his/her behavior. Or recall a time when he/she behaved well and remind him/her how good it felt to be praised for positive behavior.
constantly attending to the same child who misbehaves all day	giving him/her lots of attention when he/she is doing the right thing.
calling a student's name and then asking a question, giving no time for processing	asking the question, allowing the student to think and even share answers with another student, and then calling on a student ready to answer.

How Do You Create a Peaceful Classroom?

The concept of a peaceful classroom should be desired by every teacher. The connotation of the word *peace* brings up images of happiness and an absence of strife and problems. "A peaceable classroom or school results when the values and skills of cooperation, communication, tolerance, positive emotional expression, and conflict resolution are taught and supported throughout the culture of the school" (Girard, 1995, p. 1). This section will explore some of the practical strategies a teacher can employ in order to reach these goals.

Show Interest in Your Students

First of all, consider how you greet your students when they enter your class. Students look to the teacher's facial expressions and first words to let them know if they should feel invited into the classroom or whether they should feel that they are not welcome (Wong & Wong, 1998). Furthermore, if you are truly interested in having a peaceful classroom, you have to involve your students so that they feel like the peaceful outcome is something that they had a part in creating themselves.

Start by showing interest in them. Spend about one minute listening to them before you begin the class proceedings. Set aside a few minutes at the end of the day or class period for them to talk to you and share what's happening in their lives. Ask questions about their different cultures and allow for student expression as they contribute to individual and group assignments and projects. Students don't generally mind sharing their differences if you have created a climate of fairness and respect. Teachers need to ask sensitive questions, listen carefully to the responses, and be intentionally thoughtful as they evaluate student work, especially when this work is directly related to students' writing and talking about their own interests and experiences (Darling-Hammond, 1998). Be sure to think of the class as a group of individuals, not just a group.

Clearly Communicate What You Want and Expect

Research repeatedly points to student success when teachers clearly communicate what is expected of students. To maximize understanding, start by treating all of your students as fairly and consistently as possible. Remember that sometimes the planned rules won't work. Teachers need to excel in the areas of adaptability and flexibility. They need to be constantly analyzing, reflecting on their practices, assessing the effects of their teaching, and finally refining and improving their instructional strategies in order to continuously evaluate how students are thinking and understanding in their classes (Darling-Hammond, 1998). There may be circumstances beyond the teacher's (or the student's) control that make it very difficult to follow the everyday rules. Working with students of all ages means the teacher will have to be flexible much of the time.

Be Objective, Not Judgmental

Teachers will have more success with achieving peaceful management outcomes when they learn to be objective rather than judgmental. Whenever possible, look at a situation from the student's perspective. Sometimes, you may miss the most obvious cause of student behaviors, frustrations, or reactions if you jump to a fast conclusion. Teachers should take the time to understand before enforcing heavy consequences. If the time cannot be taken right away to do so, it may be appropriate to tell the student you want to revisit the situation later privately before discussing the consequence.

Let Them See That You Are Human

One of the most important life skills students can learn is how to make mistakes, identify them as mistakes, and learn from them. The teacher can be a powerful ally in learning this life skill. The teacher can model how to reflect on work and identify a mistake made. Sometimes the mistake is obvious, but other times it is a matter of reflecting on how a better choice could have been made. The teacher needs to model how to graciously accept imperfection. The students need to see various methods for correcting mistakes, such as apologizing, doing the extra work to redo an activity, and making a plan not to make the same mistakes in the future. A great content area to demonstrate these skills is writing. Using samples of your own writing, model the thinking process behind improving writing when you know a mistake has been made or when your best work is not represented in the finished product.

Spend a Lot of Time Among Your Students

Not only does a teacher's desk provide a barrier between students and the teacher, it can send the message that the teacher does not take an active interest in how students are processing the learning of content if the teacher is constantly seated at his/her desk during all instructional time. The most effective teachers spend a lot of time among the students while learning is taking place. While presenting information, the teacher can walk around to check that students are taking the right notes and recording the most important things. During independent work, the teacher monitors progress. During group activities, the teacher monitors tasks. The teacher is actively encouraging, directing, and adjusting the lesson according to how the students are working. In these efforts, the teacher is actively pursuing peaceful management and flow through activities in the classroom.

Work to Get Buy-In From the Students

Teachers are constantly pressured to meet the rising demands of content standards and pacing charts. Therefore, they are often tempted to rush through their content in the attempt to reach all of the goals. When students are confused or do not understand, the teacher may not even be aware of it until final assessments are made. This is frustrating for students and for teachers. The frustration can lead to behavioral problems. Therefore, a teacher's lessons will run more smoothly if he/she can find ways to get students to connect with the lesson from the beginning. For this reason, the teacher needs to work to get buy-in from them.

"Students engage in learning when they recognize a connection between what they know and the learning experience" (Diaz-Rico & Weed, 2002, p. 124). At the beginning of each lesson, the teacher will need to assess a student's prior knowledge, or what he/she already knows about the coming subject. This not only guides the teacher's instruction, but it also facilitates the students accessing their own knowledge. The teacher then provides any background knowledge needed. When there is very little prior knowledge, the teacher uses scaffolding techniques to help students build schemas, "that is, construct a framework of concepts that show the relationships of old and new learning and how they are connected" (Diaz-Rico & Weed, 2002, p. 125). This whole process allows students to connect what they already know with what they are going to learn for true learning associations.

During lessons, teachers can preplan opportunities to give the students as much choice as possible. When they are finished with a task, the teacher can provide avenues to plan what they will work on next. When possible, the teacher can put a list of activities on the board so that the students know what's expected for the day.

Another way to create this buy-in experience is to give students a purpose for everything they will be learning. Ineffective teachers keep the assignment a mystery until they announce that it has to be done and only teach according to the textbook (Wong & Wong, 1998), rather than creating dynamic learning experiences surrounding the content standards with all the resources available. Teachers easily tell students what they need to learn but not always why they need to learn it.

When a teacher actively pursues positive results regarding student success, odds increase that this will be the result (Wong & Wong, 1998). If a teacher is striving to achieve a positive room environment, then it is vital that the teacher celebrates with students when they have achieved it. Keeping open discussion on good attitudes (both teacher and students), praise when deserved, and positive reinforcement all around can work wonders. Keep in mind that simple praise can become counterproductive and is not enough to create a positive learning environment. The end result comes from a teacher who prepares purposefully, praises deserving students, positively reinforces at key moments, and maintains an upbeat attitude through the tedious parts of each school day. This teacher demonstrates to students the value of such things as effort, hard work, kindness, and dependability above and beyond simply desiring correct and neat work.

Chapter 2 Reflection

1. What physical components in your classroom contribute to a positive learning environment?

____

____

____

2. What emotional components in your classroom contribute to a positive learning environment?

____

____

____

3. Describe the importance of lowering a student's affective filter.

____

____

____

4. Identify four ways that you can change your own learning environment or instructional strategies in order to make it more positive.

____

____

____

____

____

____

Preparing Your Classroom for Success

Teachers are continually challenged to provide the best education for today's youth. What used to be standard is no longer "up to standards." In the current educational system, the rigors and demands placed on students continually increase. What a kindergarten student is asked to do at the end of the year is considerably more than what kindergartners were expected to be able to do five or ten years ago. This places an increasingly difficult undertaking on teachers who are preparing students to meet the rising demands of content standards and curriculum and also addressing the many discipline issues that arise throughout the daily lessons. Additionally, what used to work may not work anymore because the makeup of students has changed so much. Across the country, all types of social services are finding the need to respond differently to the changing population base. Teachers now often find themselves mismatched with their students in language and cultural expectations and norms. Some teachers are not changing their teaching techniques and management systems, even when the students' backgrounds and needs clearly are changing over time. Teachers may need to alter their own methods in order to reach the changing learning needs of diverse students from varying backgrounds and cultural norms in a single classroom. Teachers need to evaluate current instructional delivery methods, as well as current rules and consequences used for classroom management in order to meet the varied needs of the specific students who are sitting in their classrooms today.

Establishing Initial Expectations in Planning Standards of Conduct

There are many things teachers can do to create excellent learning situations. Ron Clark, Disney's Teacher of the Year in 2001 and author of *The Essential 55* (2003), believes that setting up expectations for acceptable behavior at the beginning of the year is one of the most important things teachers can do. A teacher's classroom management skills establish and maintain an environment where students are eager to learn under his/her guidance. Sometimes, teachers get caught in a cycle of complaint about their workload or even specific students. While such venting can help teachers feel better temporarily, unquestionably an active action plan for change is longer-lasting and far more productive. Certainly, the best way to increase the odds of success is to plan and prepare.

As you formulate a plan for your own classroom, think through the things that are important to you. At the same time, prepare yourself to keep learning and to be flexible, because just when you think you have achieved order in your class, something new will come along and catch you by surprise. Teachers must pursue the best research-based strategies with confidence in order to become effective classroom managers. Before the first student walks into your classroom each day, take some time to think about what content will be covered, what materials will be needed, and in what activities the students will be participating. As you prepare, imagine your students interacting with the texts, materials, activities, and peers around them. Try to foresee what problems might arise and make a plan for how you will address them. Write down a series of actions you might take with various problems. As you read the next section about establishing rules, consequences, and rewards, think through your own plan of action.

Establishing Standards of Conduct

Letting the entire class know the set of expectations is the key to having a successful educational day. Establishing standards should be done the first day you meet your students. According to Wong and Wong (1998), "What you do on the first days of school will determine your success or failure for the rest of the school year" (p. 3). You will need to be firm, fair, and consistent. Setting reasonable limits and consequences with consistent enforcement is essential in maintaining a safe and orderly learning environment. The rules need to be set in very specific behavioral terms. Start by thinking through your priorities, or "must-have behaviors." Post and teach these rules so that everyone knows exactly what is expected. Have the students agree to the posted rules and consequences plan by actually signing the agreement on a large poster in the room, as well as signing a send-home copy or a copy that is kept in a folder. Send the agreement home to parents so that you can implement parental collaboration and cooperation. All students need and expect clear direction and predictability, which provides a safer and more secure learning environment. A disciplinary surprise is usually not only ineffective, but it often results in the students perceiving the teacher as being unfair and unreasonable.

Classroom Rules

We have rules in every aspect of life—that is what makes civilization possible. Rules for your students are those simple things that make your classroom manageable. In order to be effective, rules should be introduced on the first day of class, and the teacher should continue to teach and reinforce them throughout the school year. Engaging your students in establishing overall classroom rules and procedures is often a successful way to encourage student involvement (Marzano, Marzano, & Pickering, 2003). However, students must understand that they cannot negotiate with schoolwide rules or classroom policies essential for managing the learning process, such as care of classroom equipment and attentiveness (Wong & Wong, 1998). It is essential to evaluate the method you choose to create and post rules, as well as the rules themselves for grade-level appropriateness. Think about your class rules as you look over this section.

First, make sure your list of rules reflects your philosophy of education. You have seen the benefits of students explaining their work to peers, so you might decide that you want them to be allowed to share their work and ask each other questions under specific conditions. On the other hand, you may determine that you want their full attention when you or anyone else is speaking to the class. You may also want them to be quiet and remain in their seats during class discussions or lectures but offer the possibility of more movement for cooperative learning activities with peer interaction for maximum academic language exposure and use. With all this in mind, two appropriate classroom rules are: "Listen and stay seated when someone is speaking" and "Use a quiet voice during cooperative learning time." When deciding on classroom rules, make sure they are easily understood, specific, and behavioral. It is best to make sure that the total set of rules is limited to five or six, at the most, and that they are generally phrased in a positive tone. This means that your list does not begin with a lot of *don'ts*. However, sometimes a rule that begins in the negative way, such as "no fighting on the playground" can be more understandable and incontestable (Wong & Wong, 1998).

Lastly, do not include common classroom procedures in the official set of classroom rules. Rules are concerned with how students behave and are tied to consequences and rewards; procedures relate to how things are done, without being tied to penalties or rewards (Wong & Wong, 1998). For example, your specific routine for bathroom use during instructional time is a procedure, not a rule with consequences. Establishing effective classroom procedures will be discussed later in Chapter 5.

In Table 3.1, there are examples of common classroom rules to get you thinking about rules to enforce in your classroom. Please note that this set of rules is not meant to be used as is; rather, choose a few rules that might apply to your classroom and create your own that fit your classroom situation. Keep in mind that too many rules can cause confusion or frustration ("Managing Inappropriate Behavior," 1990). Some of the rules are simply a different way to verbalize the same concept, and you would not want such repetition in your chosen classroom rules.

Table 3.1: Examples of Specific Classroom Rules

Work quietly without disturbing others.
When the teacher is talking, it's your turn to listen.
Raise your hand and wait to be called on before speaking.
Keep your hands, legs, and other objects to yourself.
Always walk in the halls and classroom.
Follow directions.
Be in your seat when the bell rings.
Bring all necessary supplies to class.
Use the appropriate voice level in the classroom.
Put your trash in the trash can.

Table 3.2 highlights some of the criteria a teacher should consider before formulating a set of classroom rules. These criteria might also be shared with students if you have opted to include students in the process of creating the classroom rules for the year.

Table 3.2: Criteria for Choosing Classroom Rules

Choose rules you can enforce.
Choose rules about which you feel strongly.
Choose rules that are age-appropriate.
Choose rules that encompass many actions.
Choose rules that reinforce school rules.

The following blank table provides you with space to use the examples and criteria in order to write a set of additional classroom rules. You might find that you will use the rules you already have in place and you might decide to make a few changes. Write down at least ten rules that are different from those provided in Table 3.1. Refer to all of these rules when trying to narrow down your classroom rules for the year.

More Possible Classroom Rules:

1. ______________________________
2. ______________________________
3. ______________________________
4. ______________________________
5. ______________________________
6. ______________________________
7. ______________________________
8. ______________________________
9. ______________________________
10. ______________________________

Logical and Natural Consequences for Student Behavior

Students should expect natural and logical consequences to their behavioral choices. All people need feedback in relation to appropriate and inappropriate behavior (Marzano, Marzano, & Pickering, 2003). Natural consequences are those that result directly from a student's behavior or action. An example of a natural consequence is when a student has to redo a paper if he/she loses it. Logical consequences are those the teacher deems appropriate, such as missing five minutes of recess if a student talks out of turn (Eby, Herrell, & Jordan, 2005). Ideally, the consequences should always be linked to the offense, but in all cases they should be closely aligned to the severity of the behavior. Consequences must be age-appropriate as well. All students need to understand that if they choose to disregard or violate classroom expectations, a correlation exists between their choices and the natural outcomes. When consequences are clearly posted, this connection between the decision to violate a rule and the appropriate consequence will seem more reasonable to the student. When students can make this connection, they will be better able to choose appropriate behaviors in the future (Wong & Wong, 1998).

Think through appropriate consequences before the school year begins. Make sure the consequences are logical and natural. If a student draws on his/her desk, the natural consequence is that he/she would have to clean it up during break time. It is important to discuss the natural consequences in order to help the student make the connection between his/her choice and the natural process of cause and effect. While you do not need a specific posted rule for each possible act of misbehavior, it is a good idea to have a rule that incorporates many so that you can point to the rule and then enact a logical consequence. In the example above, the rule could be "Take care of school and classroom property." Much misbehavior could fall under this one rule.

It is difficult to identify in advance appropriate disciplinary consequences for every circumstance that might arise in a school environment. Usual disciplinary consequences include: loss of a privilege, loss of free time, or a call to the parents or guardian. Any chosen consequence must also be an acceptable practice at the school, with principal approval. For example, some schools do not allow students to be kept longer than a predetermined amount of time after school. A student who has to take a school bus home should not be required to miss that bus unless the teacher has made an arrangement with a parent beforehand. A referral to the office usually comes only after other disciplinary strategies have failed to bring about the desired result. A referral is only going to work if the office has a procedure set up to deal with referred students. You would not want to send a student to the office only to have him/her sit there ignored all day or returned to your classroom without any administrative intervention given. Severe violations that result in the child being sent to the principal or vice principal may include fighting, possession of drugs or weapons, physical threats, sexual harassment, and constant disruption or direct defiance.

Positive Consequences and Rewards

The term *consequences* often makes teachers think of negative consequences for misbehavior. However, the meaning should include consequences for all behavior; thus, positive behavior should bring about positive consequences as well. All corrective intervention programs need to include a healthy balance between negative consequences for inappropriate behavior and positive consequences for expected behavior (Marzano, Marzano, & Pickering, 2003). Students, like adults, respond to positive reinforcement better than to sarcasm or use of constant negative chastisement. Praising desired behavior is usually much more effective than reactive discipline and punishment. Nevertheless, positive reinforcement needs to be specific and descriptive, earned, and accurate.

Praise is only one component in a classroom rewards system. There is some research that discourages the use of rewards in general, as it has been found that students become more interested in getting the reward rather than changing behavior in a positive direction. Therefore, there needs to be the focused component in the overall management system to teach children how to take responsibility for actions and internalize positive values (Kohn, 1994).

However, most teachers use some form of rewards in their classrooms. These rewards should be a reflection of previously established classroom expectations. Your praise communicates to your students what you really care about. If you give praise for work that looks nice, you might get students who aim for that simplified goal and not delve further into the actual skills that you are ultimately aiming to enforce, such as descriptive writing or proper sentence format. Effort and growth is generally what you are after, and you should concentrate your comments in this direction. Give explicit feedback immediately, because students generally need to know when they are doing something correctly at that moment. Rewards, like consequences, should be in proportion to students' correct choices. They should have a legitimate educational purpose, and the return offered should be sufficient to motivate the child to continue making correct decisions. Contingent rewards are privileges or favored activities earned by following the rules and performing well in other areas ("Managing Inappropriate Behavior," 1990).

Reflect on who earns rewards. While some earn rewards for doing great things, others might earn rewards for not doing negative things ("Managing Inappropriate Behavior," 1990). Consider various levels of rewards. There might be *individual* praise or rewards for individual behavior, such as choice time during centers, stamps on a paper, or choice in a partner with whom to work. There might be *group* cooperation points where, at the end of the week, the table with the most points gets to choose a prize or receive the ability to choose an activity the following week. There might also be a *whole-class* reward when the entire class is participating well in a lesson, such as accomplishing a project in order to eat lunch in the classroom with the teacher. Finally, establish your system of praise and rewards in a way that is genuine and in line with who you are. In other words, be authentic and sincere.

Most importantly, in this area, keep reflective records to document whether your particular system of consequences and rewards is working to manage the classroom and general learning environment. Effective teachers need to maintain a record-keeping system that allows them to keep track of student behavior in an efficient manner without wasting too much instructional time (Marzano, Marzano, & Pickering, 2003). Explore other options with patience and flexibility or combine approaches for the most effective learning environment ("Managing Inappropriate Behavior," 1990). In order to inspire your flow of ideas, walk around the school and take pictures of evidence of rules, consequences, and rewards in other classrooms. This will help you decide what you want to include in your classroom and how you want to convey your expectations clearly to your students.

Getting Students' Attention With Signals

Students are not learning if they are not listening. When a teacher needs to cut through the chatter in order to get the students' attention, the teacher's voice isn't always the best tool. The use of a signal can be an effective tool. This is an action or prop that is used to obtain student attention. An orchestra conductor does this by tapping the baton to get the musicians to stop and pay attention. Teachers can do the same thing with a gesture or sound. There are as many of these signals as your imagination can invent; or ask your peers for some of their best ideas and find one or more that you like. Ultimately, you have to find out what works best for you and your students. Make sure it is age-appropriate. A signal that is highly effective for elementary-level students may be childish and demeaning for middle and high school students. For example, many students associate the typical bell with the lower grades and might feel disrespected if it is used in their classroom. You can consider a song or a chant. One elementary teacher would calmly say, "We are. . ." and the class would respond with "room 9 winners" and then turn to face the teacher. This can add to a sense of belonging in the classroom. As one teacher recalls, a younger sibling of one of her students excitedly told her, "I'm in your class next year and I already know what to say!" He went on to report that he knew the classroom mantra and was excited to use it. You can consider counting backwards to convey the expected period of time in which to accomplish a task, clean up, or move. Perhaps a rain stick, a small gong, or a series of claps will work for your classroom. Often students react better to a quiet sound rather than a loud one. Establish expectations for how fast you expect the class to react to your signal and reward the class with praise when they respond appropriately.

Some teachers use several signals, each one used for a different task. Examples are a train whistle to get students to line up, a hotel bell to let group leaders know to collect supplies for their group members, and a timer to give a five-minute warning. When you are ready to address your students, give the signal and then wait for the class to be completely silent. When using a signal for group transitions, make sure you give your students a chance to think before you require them to do something. Give the signal, which instructs them to be silent, inform them that you expect them to sit quietly while you give the instructions, and tell them that you will give the signal again (or a different signal) when they are permitted to move to the next activity.

New teachers may not realize that everything they want students to learn, including the procedures mentioned in this chapter, must be explicitly taught and practiced, especially with younger children. Successful teachers give expectations, instruct students on the procedures, and offer plenty of opportunities to practice before they expect the students to actually be successful in using a procedure efficiently in their daily routine. Teachers with highly organized and well-managed classrooms realize that students often forget procedures and need to practice frequently, especially after returning from the weekend or a longer school break. Whichever signal you choose to use, the key is to model and practice until it is a natural behavior on the students' part. It is important to give the students time to rehearse the procedure and for the teacher to consistently use the signal to reinforce the skill (Wong & Wong, 1998).

Always be upfront about your expectations and don't make students guess what you are trying to accomplish. A signal is not any good if your class does not know to respond to it. Decide if you are going to have a visual or auditory signal, or a combination of both. Decide how the students should demonstrate that they have heard your signal. For example, if you clap, should they clap too, or should they put down their pencils and look up? Sometimes, a silent teacher signal and a quiet reminder can be equally strategic (Starr, 2005).

You should consider different types of signals to find out what seems right for you and fits your teaching style. The first thing to remember is that it needs to sound different from the students' voices. If you want it to be successful, your students need to be able to see or hear it from anywhere in the room. One of the most common times to use a signal is when your class will be working in cooperative groups. They will need to be able to hear it even when many of them are talking at the same time. Remember, you may be anywhere in the room when you want to use your signal. Make sure it is convenient to you at all times. Since you might be using this signal many times during the day, pick something that doesn't become bothersome to hear over and over again.

Table 3.3 shows some signals that you could use in your classroom. The list is separated into visual and auditory signals. Some of the suggestions could be combined. The teacher might consider one teacher signal to get attention and one student signal to show they are ready for further instruction.

Table 3.3: Possible Classroom Signals

Visual Signals

- Turn lights on and off quickly
- Red light
- Hold up your hand and wait
- Thumbs up

Auditory Signals

- Squeaky toys
- Tap on wind chimes or xylophone
- Create a classroom chant
- Count backwards from five
- Small bell
- Hotel bell
- Hold up rain stick and shake it
- Clap your hands twice while the students mimic your clap
- Hold up one hand and slowly count to three

Effective Room Arrangements

To make sure you are able to make the best of your classroom discipline and classroom management systems, you need to plan how your room will work. From the very beginning, you want to establish a climate of work. This means you need to consider the floor space, desk arrangements, work area for students, wall space, access to materials, and teacher space (Wong & Wong, 1998). Decide from the onset to be flexible. The students will appreciate hearing that if one plan isn't working for the whole class, then changes can be made. Many teachers who use group arrangements change groups as often as every month. This way, they can reassure those who aren't getting along with their group members that the change is coming soon. Many students appreciate a new group or fresh perspectives and faces at least a few times during the year. Think through the activity flow when the room is filled with students. Check to see that there is plenty of room for everyone to move around.

Think about the location in the room from where you generally teach. Some teachers use an overhead machine, a computer projection screen, or a whiteboard to which students will need to have visual access. Consider your ability to easily reach what you need. Reflect on how students will access paper and pencils and other supplies. Consider your teaching style and whether you plan many interactive and group activities. Teachers of younger children may want to consider room for floor activities. Teachers who use rotation centers may want to consider room for various stations around the room. Teachers who have many students but who still like to have group activities might consider training students to quickly rearrange their desks from lecture position to group position. If students commonly work in groups at computers, perhaps having them all lumped in one corner is not the most efficient way to arrange them. Awkward situations become time-consuming, so make sure you can easily get into the bookshelves and cabinets.

Next, make sure your students can readily see instructional displays and presentations. To accomplish this, it is a good idea to have everyone facing forward for maximum focus during direct instruction time. You don't want to create pockets where students can hide from teacher supervision. Even with these limitations, you have choices about how you arrange desks. They can be put in rows, circles, semicircles, or small groups. Whatever the plan, it should be a well-thought-out reflection of your teaching style and practices. If you are a teacher who includes a lot of cooperative work, then putting your students in pods may work very well for you. Think through the characteristics and needs of your class and plan accordingly. If you have a combination class, do you want the grades separated or integrated? Are there students with special needs who need to be situated toward the front or back of the classroom?

Consider the effects that the physical arrangement of the room will have on developing the type of classroom environment you want. Rows of desks suggest order and discipline but do little to build a sense of community. However, rows accommodate large numbers of students and can often be quickly moved into group settings. Communication and cooperation among groups of students are best facilitated by putting them in clusters or pods. Large or concentric circle arrangements encourage communication and sharing among the entire class. The seating arrangement can be changed as often as you'd like, but remember to continually coach the students about your expectations and to give them practice moving appropriately in any new classroom arrangement. Tell them the purpose for your classroom arrangement so that they can share your vision of a well-organized flow that facilitates their important learning process.

While it may appear old-fashioned to many, some teachers prefer that their students sit in rows, and there is nothing inherently wrong with this approach. The truth is that this method might work very well for you if your students are acting out while sitting in groups or circles. Sometimes it works well at the beginning of the school year to minimize distractions and allow easy monitoring while you become familiar with the students in your class (Wong & Wong, 1998). Sometimes just getting them to pay attention and limiting their interactions is what you need. Keep in mind that while rows of desks provide an advantage in keeping order, they leave little space for activities.

On pages 68 and 69, you will find two sample room arrangements. Examine them closely and then complete the activity on page 70. See how these two different room plans can help you decide what would be right for your classroom.

Classroom Arrangement 1

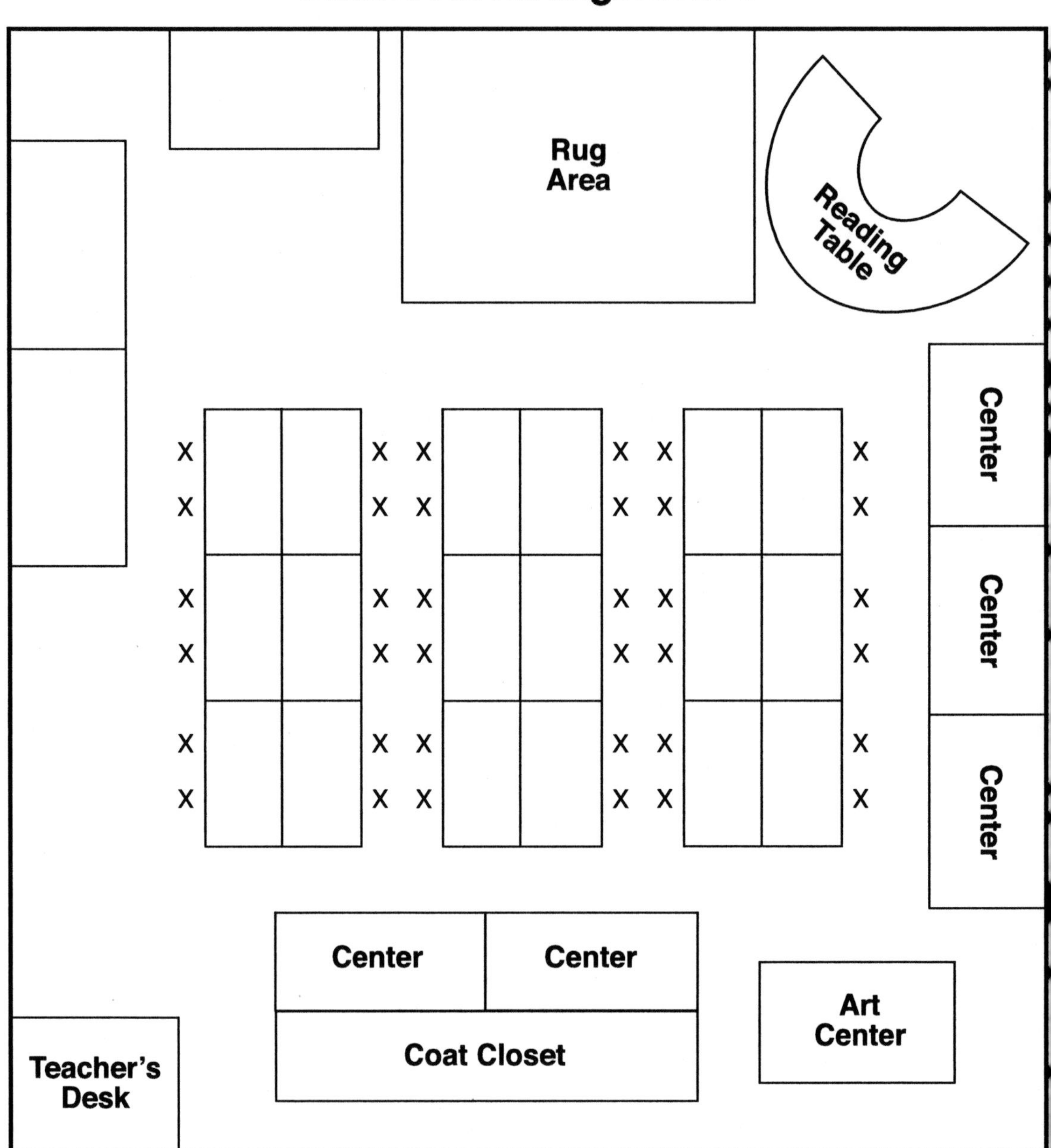

Classroom Arrangement 2

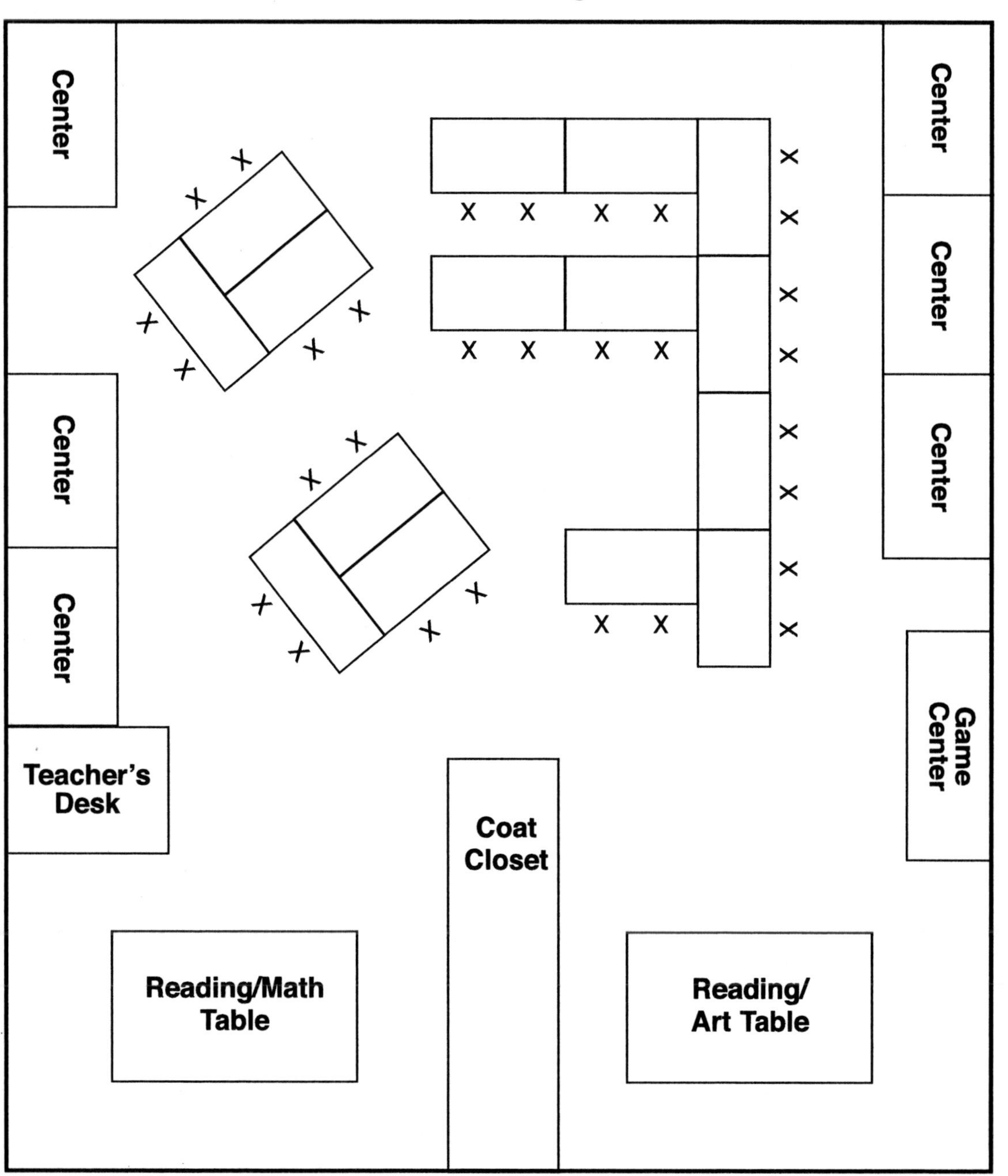

You Be the Judge

1. How well do these two room arrangements work? What works and what doesn't work in them?

____

____

____

____

____

2. Do the teacher and students have plenty of room to move around in each of the plans?

____

3. Can the teacher see every student at all times in each of the plans?

____

4. Can the students easily see instructional displays and presentations?

____

5. Which plan is your favorite and why? What would you change?

____

____

____

____

____

____

Teaching is a profession that never remains static for long. It is exciting and exhausting at the same time, because there are always new things to learn and ways to improve your craft. Something that worked beautifully with one class may flop with another. Each year provides a new opportunity for you to reflect on your current challenges and successes. It is important to remember that with rules, procedures, and a system of consequences and rewards in place, the teacher can increase the amount of time the students are working, which directly works toward increasing actual learning (Wong & Wong, 1998). With that in mind, you will need to constantly reflect on the expectations that you have conveyed, the rules you have established, the consequences for abiding by or not abiding by the rules, and the ways that you facilitate the entire management system in order to determine how well you have prepared your class for success.

Chapter 3 Reflection

1. Outline some classroom rules, consequences and rewards you might plan to use in the coming year. Are these different from those you already have in place this year?

2. What problems do you foresee or already have present in your current classroom with the rules and consequences plan that you wrote down?

3. How can you establish logical and natural consequences?

4. Describe how your room arrangement helps or hinders effective instructional time in your classroom.

Keeping All Students on Task

In any classroom, there will be students who find almost anything more interesting than the subject at hand. These children may not see the relevance of the lesson, they might be bored, or they may have anxiety about the work or other situations in their lives. This can be very challenging when teachers feel constant pressure to produce good learners and raise test scores. While it may be unrealistic to expect every teacher to have every student working to full potential every second of the day, in this chapter, teachers will explore various strategies necessary for keeping more students on task for more of the instructional time. As you read through the ideas, seek ways to hook students into a lesson with beginning anticipatory sets that use approaches such as humor, questions, startling facts, or stories. Teachers are in competition with everything children hear and see, so they have to rise to the challenge. The challenge to engage the students' attention can be especially difficult when teachers are presenting something new. Therefore, this chapter will explore presenting new material in the ways that students learn best, as well as allowing plenty of time for practice, and then finally, letting them process what they have learned before moving on to the next concept.

Student Engagement Starts With Well-Planned Lessons

This chapter explores how teachers can pull students to be actively engaged and on task during instructional time. The starting place for this discussion has to be the teacher's planning and preparation. There are many models of lesson planning that can help teachers plan lessons. Research is clear that the most effective teachers minimize wasted time and maximize the time that students are actively engaged in learning (Echevarria, Vogt, and Short, 2004). The following list is not exhaustive, but it offers support in ensuring that lessons are well-planned.

- Teachers start with established content standards. They are teaching to required content standards rather than just teaching through a given textbook.
- Teachers plan realistic objectives that can be met by most of the students in a class period.
- Before the lesson, materials are gathered and preparation for lesson activities is completed.
- Teachers plan to engage students by anticipatory activities that connect their prior knowledge to the content they will be learning and creating excitement for the activity.
- The lesson includes direct instruction, teacher modeling, and opportunities for the teacher

to check that students understand. Time and flexibility are allotted for necessary review or reteaching.

- The students are given the chance to practice and apply skills and new knowledge practice activities with teacher support, as well as independent practice.
- The teacher brings closure to the lesson and ties in key concepts to the overall unit of study.
- The end product of the lesson matches the planned objective and the practice that the students engaged in during the lesson.
- Students are informally or formally assessed on their abilities to accomplish the objective.
- The lesson covers the four domains of language for a wider breadth of practice, using reading, writing, speaking, and listening activities.
- Interactive activities are planned to allow for student engagement.
- Materials are appropriate to age and ability levels, or they are adapted so that they are comprehensible.

Once a teacher is actively incorporating many of these components in daily lesson planning, the teacher may find that students are naturally working more on task simply because there is not time to be engaged in other activities. However, problems will still occur, and the rest of the chapter will explore some ideas for addressing the need for all students to be engaged in learning.

Learning Modalities

One of the ways that teachers keep students actively engaged in lessons is by careful planning and lesson preparation as it relates to the best ways to address the students' individualized learning needs. The teacher needs to plan and prepare the actual activities and materials that will be used during each lesson with these needs in mind. *Learning modalities* is a concept that helps explain how humans learn.

It is necessary first to differentiate the commonly used terms *learning styles* and *learning modalities*. While the term *learning styles* emphasizes differences in temperament, attitude, and preferred manner of accomplishing a task, the term *learning modalities* is more specific to the methods in assessment or instruction that deal with the auditory, visual, or tactile possibilities for learning that are dependent upon each individual student (Lokerson, 1992). Learning styles refer to the individual preferences in processing information, but learning modalities refer to the actual ways students acquire knowledge (Diaz-Rico & Weed, 2002). Students have different favored learning styles, so teachers should present information through different modalities and offer multiple opportunities for students to practice and apply new knowledge through listening, speaking, reading, and writing activities, thus achieving the ability to meet student needs and further both language and content development (Echevarria, Vogt, & Short, 2004).

The students enter the room with their established learning styles. Therefore, this section will explore how the teacher can meet those varied styles with the inclusion of an appropriate plan for learning modalities in lesson planning. There are three basic methods for taking in information—visual, auditory, and kinesthetic. Almost everyone uses some combination of all three methods, but most people learn best through one favored modality. When this is kept in mind and lesson delivery is varied to include all three modalities, then it becomes much easier for the students to pay attention and, as a result, teaching is much more efficient and effective.

Visual Learners

This modality describes the majority of learners. Visual learners receive and retain new information more efficiently if they can *see* it. They can usually remember what was seen and then can visually reproduce it. They do best if they see the big picture and purpose right off the bat. Teachers can help the visual learners in their classes by using colorful pictures or graphics. Chalkboards, overhead projectors, models, and demonstrations are other effective visuals. When teachers use in-class demonstrations, photographs, flip charts with colorful markers, and handouts, they are making it much easier for the majority of the students to quickly grasp content concepts. Even though most students tend to be visual learners, many teachers continue to teach by speaking or lecturing, and yet they still expect students to learn by simply listening. This compounds the issue even further for English language learners, who are trying to not only learn content but connect it to concepts that they have learned, or are developing, in their primary languages. Visual reference will allow them to connect the new learning to a visual representation.

Visual teaching strategies don't happen by accident; the teacher needs to carefully plan which concepts will be important to show visually in order for students to better comprehend the overall content. Then the teacher needs to thoughtfully pull together the appropriate materials and visuals. For some students, the teacher will need to limit visual confusion and unnecessary visual stimuli, keeping visuals of only the essential concepts in sight (Echevarria, Vogt, & Short, 2004). For example, often an entire film on a subject offers many unnecessary visuals and concepts. It can also waste valuable class time. If the teacher displays only the portion of the film that will visually display and explain the most important concepts, the students can watch it and continue with the lesson activities with the visual representation attached to the key concepts. The teacher can also strengthen student skills by guiding them through visualizing concepts in their heads. This will help students to begin to independently "create" visuals when they are reading texts that are not supported visually.

The possibilities are endless. It is most effective to start with *realia*, or real concrete objects to show. When this is not possible, the next most effective strategies include showing photographs, pictures, and parts of movies and films. Finally, even more abstract graphic organizers or attached small illustrations to important key vocabulary can do wonders for visual learners.

Auditory Learners

These students need to hear the information you are presenting so their brains can connect it to previously understood concepts. They retrieve information from the "tape recorder" in their heads exactly as they heard it. They can also mimic tone and pitch. Hearing information in creative tones and quality can be beneficial for their retention of material, as well as being able to attach appropriate sounds to concepts. They learn best from lectures and by repeating information out loud or explaining it to others. Auditory learners of all ages benefit from repeating and rehearsing information in chants, songs, and creative voices. Study groups are highly effective for auditory learners. While merely having access to text might be difficult for them, they can be best included in the learning of textual content through audio tapes, lectures, collaborative groups, and paraphrasing. Teachers can also reach these students with question-and-answer times, debates, reading aloud, and discussions. A major role for teachers is to set up authentic learning situations where students are engaging in real communication as they learn content (Diaz-Rico & Weed, 2002).

Kinesthetic (Hands-On) Learners

Other students learn best through experience and actions. Beyond textual reading and teacher lecturing, these learners need to experience the content through well-planned instructional activities and well-chosen materials that convey the content concepts most effectively. They remember their feelings and an overall impression of the information. They might not easily visualize a story in their minds but, rather, associate classroom experiences with the emotions they felt at the time. Kinesthetic learners like to physically manipulate objects and classroom materials in order to grasp the information. Traditionally, teachers rarely address the kinesthetic modality in grades above the primary level. In the planning of extra materials or interactive learning activities, addressing this modality can make the teacher overwhelmed with the preparation or feel less in control over what happens. However, teachers need to strive to involve the kinesthetic students by letting them put projects together, draw or sketch their ideas, touch an artifact, or operate something.

The inclusion of hands-on materials, such as manipulatives, gives students more opportunity to practice concepts, leading to enhanced understanding (Echevarria, Vogt, & Short, 2004). Board or computer games work well with kinesthetic learners, as does having them present their own step-by-step demonstrations of concepts. In cooperative projects, the kinesthetic learners can be the ones in charge of dispersing materials. The teacher can adapt text for these learners by allowing them to have the information on cards that they can then move around and sort by sequence or comparison in order to better comprehend what they have read. Again, the options are only limited by teacher creativity. Once the key lesson concepts are identified, the teacher needs to decide which materials and activities will allow these learners to retain the necessary information in order to be successful in learning the content.

In which of the three methods (visual, auditory, kinesthetic) do you do the least amount of instruction?

____

____

____

I can improve my instructional strategies in this area by _______________

____

____

____

Appropriate Use of Instructional Time and Procedures

Another important aspect when discussing student engagement is the evaluation of actual instructional delivery and planned instructional time. There is a high correlation between the appropriate level of difficulty in the students' work and their behavior. If the assignment is too difficult, students may become frustrated, give up, and begin to act out. Conversely, if the assignement is too easy, students become bored and often fill the time with negative behavior. Before a lesson, teachers need to plan realistic learning goals to meet the day's objectives. During the lesson, teachers need to constantly monitor student learning by walking around the classroom and checking for student understanding. Then they adjust the lesson and adapt the pace in order to meet the needs of the students for learning the appropriate concepts. After a lesson, teachers need to assess whether the lesson objectives were met and whether concepts need to be reviewed or retaught in different ways.

Theorists have given this concept of teacher effectiveness several names, depending on their viewpoints. The term *Constructivism* refers to the teacher's ability to analyze students' understandings and ways of learning and then customize the teaching approach to fit their learning styles (Brooks & Brooks, 1999). The term *withitness* refers to a teacher who is paying attention to more than one thing at a time (Eby, Herrell, & Jordan, 2005). The label is not as important as the awareness of what is going on in the class and the flexibility to adjust and differentiate the lesson according to the individualized needs of the students. Students need academically engaging time in which teachers are prepared, have strong management skills, and do not spend excessive amounts of time making announcements or passing out materials (Echevarria, Vogt, & Short, 2004). While walking around the classroom, the teacher needs to be actively assisting students who are having trouble adjusting to the level of difficulty of the work. This will go a long way to ensure proper classroom management. Providing help to those who need it and giving alternative tasks to students who have demonstrated mastery of the assignment will help to prevent boredom and classroom disruptions.

Chapter 3 already discussed the need for well-established rules in a classroom. There is also a need for recognized and practiced procedures in each classroom that will help students know when and how to accomplish various tasks during their time in the classroom. Procedures are important in society and classrooms so that people can function in an acceptable and organized manner (Wong & Wong, 1998).

Consider how much time students wait for the teacher to be prepared; it is highly effective to start instruction at the beginning of each class period or content block time, move quickly from your talking to actual learning activity, and continue the instruction/activities until the very end of the allowed time (Starr, 2005). Students who have learned procedures should not need even five minutes to get ready for a break or a recess. Often this is the time when problems arise. Procedures need to be established, taught, and practiced for starting the day or class period, dismissal, quieting the class, students seeking help, movement of students, access to supplies, and more (Wong & Wong, 1998). Marzano suggests with younger students, in particular, that the teacher practice how he/she wants them to enter the room, begin working on an assignment, turn in completed work, and line up to leave (Marzano, Marzano, & Pickering, 2003). The rest of this chapter will explore how a well set-up system of procedural knowledge prevents many of the common problems that arise in a typical classroom.

"Teacher, I'm done!"

The common utterance "Teacher, I'm done" leads to the need for planning individual work time when a student has finished the assigned task. Problems often arise during the period of time when some students have finished their work and others are completing an assignment. The teacher needs to provide a plan for extra learning activities. The teacher should introduce an approved extra activity before starting a task. The teacher might also use such extra activities for when the students enter the classroom, during which time the teacher is occupied with addressing morning concerns and collecting homework. The activity should match the content during that block of time. For example, extra activities during math time might include an extra set of math problems on the board or the freedom to explore a certain set of math manipulatives. Perhaps the teacher could ask students to follow a series of simple directions to draw a geometric figure. During language arts instruction, the teacher might post a topic sentence and have the students write three sentences related to that topic. Students could also be given the chance to work in their handwriting books or to read silently. The teacher can consider an activity chart where various independent activities are posted. When students' assigned work is completed, they can choose an extra activity. The students put their names in the slots indicating the activities in which they wish to participate. For younger students, these may include a listening center, computer time, or art activities, and they should be changed frequently to maintain interest. For any free-choice centers, the teacher will want to remind students daily of behavior expectations and consequences for disrupting the students who are still working on the assigned task.

Students out of Their Seats

To establish order, teachers should consider their teaching styles and how they want to organize procedures for the number of students they will allow out of their seats at any time. Teachers also need to consider acceptable reasons for allowing students to leave their seats. Because these decisions may change based on the type of instruction happening in the classroom, these procedures are taught to the students as routine practices rather than one specific posted rule. The procedure is going to change based on whole-group instruction and interaction activities, small-group centers or rotations, and independent work time. Simply posting a number of how many children may be out of their seats can be highly disruptive (for example, to sharpen a pencil), because then the other students are spending their learning time concentrating on when they can get up.

It is more effective to decide when students can accomplish the various things they want to do. Examples include allowing students to sharpen pencils only at the set transitions each day or offering preparation time before each activity during which students are allowed to get a piece of paper. Consider preventative procedures that save even this time; for example, have a can with sharpened pencils and a basket with extra paper that students are responsible for preparing at the end of each school day for their groups the following day. Hopefully, the teacher is planning plenty of well-planned interactive activities that allow the students to get up, share information with their peers, stretch their legs, and interact with content. Then, students will have less desire to "escape" from their seats. Normally, students should not be allowed out of their seats when the teacher is instructing the whole group or working directly with that child's assigned group.

Student Use of the Restroom and Drinking Fountains

Students are expected to get their drinks and to use the restroom during their breaks. However, there are other times when the need arises. Think through what your policy should be. Are you going to let them decide for themselves when they need to go? Is there going to be any type of consequence or record keeping for this? If they do leave the room during class time, unless unusual circumstances exist, they should go by themselves if they are mature enough. This is a procedural issue that may vary by age, school policy, campus layout, and school schedule. Be clear so that the students are aware of the expectations.

Proximity and Classroom Management

Once the teacher becomes aware of the profound potential that personal space plays in social interaction, he/she can use proximity as a very effective tool for classroom management and for keeping students engaged in lesson activities. Simply put, that means that teachers who walk around the classroom and monitor student conduct usually maintain much better classroom control than those who remain in one spot. A teacher may choose to quietly move into the student's space (one to three feet), making the teacher the authority in that proximity. It can be highly effective to give a specific classroom instruction while standing next to the student least likely to act on it. This action often diffuses the student's desire to act out during a transitional move or speak out of turn while the other students are complying with the direction. Author Fred Jones (2000) writes that the classroom is divided into three distinct areas. The nearby red zone is where the students are actively listening and involved. The yellow zone, which is usually 10 to15 feet from the teacher, is where the students may be involved when they think the teacher is watching. Finally, he calls the back of the room the green zone, where the students are playing around or daydreaming because they don't feel engaged. When the teacher moves around, boundaries are changed in these groups, and the students who were in the yellow or red zones must start to pay attention. Thus, through mobility, the teacher is constantly disrupting the students' impulse to become distracted or disturb others.

The strategy of proximity can be highly effective with the most restless students (Starr, 2005). Any time that a teacher plans an interactive activity, the teacher needs to be the most active person in the room, constantly rotating from group to group to monitor whether the students are on task and to check for student understanding in order to determine if more instruction is needed. Supervising students from the back of the classroom can also be a highly effective classroom management tool, especially during a video or independent work time.

It may also be appropriate to isolate a student from other students due to a pattern of consistent disruptive behavior. If this is the case, remember that the teacher needs to maintain visual contact and be able to directly supervise this student at all times. Try to make it as positive as possible by saying something like, "I want you to sit over here where you won't be disturbed. You are important to us." The teacher should constantly be attempting to pull a separated student into the lesson activity, whenever possible. The movement should not be a punishment; it should be a removal of distractions so that the student can continue to participate fully in the learning.

Helping Every Student Work on Task

Most of the responsibility for student learning in the classroom falls on teachers and how they plan for student engagement. They are given the task of doing as much as possible to bring the students into the learning process. With this in mind, here are some techniques teachers can try with students who are the most challenging to engage. With each type of learning challenge, the teacher will be presented with the opportunity to reflect and write down ideas for addressing these needs.

Students Who Constantly Display Minor Misbehaviors

Some unacceptable student behaviors are often best dealt with by using a technique known as extinction. This is simply ignoring minor negative behavior so it is not reinforced by providing the desired attention. This technique usually causes this negative conduct to stop. If the undesired behavior persists, the teacher will need to use more direct and forceful disciplinary intervention strategies. The teacher should model and teach the desired behavior and ignore the undesired behavior, as long as it is not interfering with other students' learning processes ("Managing Inappropriate Behavior," 1990). One of the most simple and effective solutions some teachers utilize for small reoccurring problems is to make tally marks on the board each time a student is not on task or is displaying any kind of misbehavior. The teacher explains privately to the student what the tally marks are for and then follows through without saying a word. This serves as a wonderful visual reminder and can improve behavior for certain students within a few days.

As with all disciplinary strategies, the teacher needs to remain flexible enough to recognize when a plan won't work for a certain student and an alternative plan needs to be set in place.

In my class, I can help students who constantly display minor misbehaviors by

____

____

____

Students Who Are Slow to Complete Assignments

For students who are slow to complete assignments, the teacher might need to reevaluate the amount of work assigned. Many times, a student can demonstrate competency of the concept without completing the entire page. If a student demonstrates a working knowledge of the skill, then you can accept the amount of an assignment he/she is able to complete in the time allotted. Many times, a timer works well and the assignment can be turned into a contest. Instead of just trying to finish the work, the student is trying to beat the clock, which is a lot more fun. This strategy is only effective if the teacher truly believes the student is able to complete the assignments faster than he/she is presently doing.

The teacher can also assign a peer helper for a short period. It is the peer helper's role to see that another student stays on track. If a tutor takes time to help this individual, then he/she can be rewarded by not having to turn in part of his/her own assignment. When possible, the student who works slowly may need a quiet place to work and, initially, this student may benefit from rewards for finishing an assignment within the time limit.

In my class, I can help students who are slow to complete assignments by

____

____

____

Students Who Want Constant Help

There will be certain students who seem to need constant help. For them, the first step is to make sure they understand the assignment. Once that is done, these are the students who should be given the chance to explain to the rest of the class what they are supposed to do. The teacher can also opt to have the students share their understanding of the task with a partner before beginning. The teacher needs to first meet with these students during the first few minutes of independent work and, when possible, show their work to the class when it is successfully completed. A good place for these students is often next to the teacher, so that immediate questions can be answered easily. The teacher needs to also decide if the lessons are outside these students' modalities. Observe their successes and ask how they like to learn best.

In my class I can help students who are constantly asking for help by ________

____

____

____

Students Who Consistently Finish Early

There are also those students who consistently finish their work early. Before a teacher can begin to prepare for these students, the first thing to do is to figure out why they are finished when they are. Are the students finishing the work quickly with many mistakes, finishing early because there are many students struggling with concepts, or are they finishing because the work was too easy for them? Think through what you want from them when they have finished. Will you have some extra activities or centers available? Do you have a "May Do" list of things on the board that students may do when they are finished with the "Must Do" assigned work? For these students, you might have computer sites listed or bookmarked where students can investigate topics and write a report for extra credit. Extension activities that go with each assignment are also a good idea. Finally, if students have finished all the required work, the teacher might consider giving them choices of activities, as discussed earlier. If the work is consistently too easy for certain students in your class, you will need to look into options for bright or gifted children, such as curriculum compacting with acceleration or extension activities, where you can allow these students to explore content beyond the regular coursework required by the curriculum.

In my class I can help students who consistently finish early and need something else to do by ____

____

____

____

Students Who Are Unmotivated

There are also those students who just seem unmotivated. A lack of motivation can be due to a variety of reasons, ranging from confusion to boredom. Typically, an unmotivated student doesn't look at assignments as fun or interesting. Sometimes, this will also happen when a student feels "dumb," and he/she would rather not pay attention than to attempt the assignment and fail. First, the teacher needs to make a point of validating an unmotivated student's intelligence and importance to the class. The teacher can then follow up with praise. Furthermore, the teacher can call on these students when the teacher knows they will be successful. The teacher should show an interest in these students and ask for their opinions, whenever appropriate and without embarrassing them. Again, if a certain student consistently is able to learn at a faster pace, the teacher may need to look into some of the extension strategies for gifted and bright children. Sometimes what appears to be a lack of motivation could be boredom because of the fact that students are not being challenged enough at their learning levels. Every child deserves to go through a challenging learning process as they work toward academic learning goals.

In my class I can help students who seem unmotivated by ____________________

____

____

____

Students Who Blurt Out Answers

It is easy to identify students who are impulsive and blurt out the answers. They announce themselves. This can be very disruptive if it happens over and over again. However, the sensitive teacher can turn a positive thing (a student who can't wait to be active in his/her own learning) into a positive situation for everyone. This problem actually highlights the ineffectiveness of the traditional teaching model in which a teacher asks questions and the students answer the questions. What often happens is that the teacher asks a question, the same students always answer the questions, and the rest of the students tune out and breathe a sigh of relief because they know someone else will always answer the questions. By changing teaching patterns, this problem can be eliminated.

The teacher can instead make everyone accountable by posing a question, insisting on quiet think time for everyone, and then allowing some pairing up for everyone to share answers. With this strategy, the "answer blurters" feel like they get to give their answers first, even though everyone else is also sharing answers simultaneously. The students who don't like answering questions aloud are still held accountable for coming up with the answers. Shy students or English language learners have the support of sharing with a peer and hearing the answers already given by the answer blurters, while being accountable to come up with their own answers. Some teachers will pull sticks with names out of a can for someone to share his/her answers with the whole class. Because of the extra language processing happening in the classroom, teachers will often be pleasantly surprised at the new depth of answers students give.

In times where this process is not possible, the teacher can find ways to give recognition to these students who need to blurt out answers, and then encouragement to have them allow others to feel the same. If this problem occurs in a small-group situation, try the strategy where everyone in a group is given the same number of small blocks or counting markers. As the children work on the project, they each turn in a counting marker to the center of the group each time they verbally contribute something. Once the student has no more counting markers, he/she is no longer allowed to speak until everyone else has spent all of their counter markers.

With a student who refuses to abide by these strategies, the teacher can ultimately write a contract with this student specifying exactly what behavior is expected. For a visual reminder, the teacher can keep a running tally on the board of every time this student blurts out answers inappropriately. Only the student should be aware of what the tallies signify and why they are there. The teacher may want to have a predetermined secret signal for this student for when the blurting out reoccurs. Finally, as with other student problems, be sure to communicate with the parents so they can reinforce classroom expectations at home.

In my class I can help students who are constantly blurting out answers by

____

____

____

Students Who Talk to Others During Quiet Times

There are always those students who talk to others during quiet times. This usually happens when students are excited about what they are doing, but it can also happen when they are bored or don't understand what to do. This needs to be approached in different ways, depending on the particular child and the reason why he/she is talking. First and foremost, evaluate your teaching practices. Are you allowing enough time for students to mentally and verbally process their own learning, or are you talking a majority of the time? The strategies suggested for students who blurt out answers will also be very helpful for these students. These are students who need to use language in order to remember, rehearse, and retain new information. Even if they are talking occasionally about things other than content, with the right strategies, the teacher can use their strengths toward increasing their participation in a lesson and actually discussing more content than they would have in a typical "listening-only" lesson. Also, evaluate the appropriateness of the task to find out if it is too difficult or if the time limit is too short or too long. Once you have made sure the assignment is clearly understood, then praise or reward those who are working quietly.

There are certainly times when students need to listen to the teacher or work quietly during independent work. Many times, if they are given an initial chance to share orally with a peer about what their plan is, they will then get right to work because they have had the chance to share. Sometimes, the only thing the teacher can do is to separate these students from the others. If you need to do this, do it as positively as possible by saying something like, "Please create an office for yourself in the back of the room. I don't want anyone to disturb you while you are working." Be sure to give these students frequent opportunities for interaction. Again, this is not a punishment but a strategy to solve a problem, so always allow separated students to participate in lessons when they are willing to do so within the expected guidelines. Finally, reward successes with something like a scheduled time for a special activity of their choice.

In my class I can help students who talk a lot during quiet time by __________

____

____

____

Trying to understand the motivation behind a student's actions can be a very difficult task. Interpreting the actions of learners and shaping their academic experiences requires knowledge of child development and understanding growth along cognitive, social, physical, and emotional domains (Darling-Hammond, 1998). There is so much going in a typical classroom situation, but once a teacher thinks he/she knows why students are behaving in such a manner, what then? If the problem is common among many students, it may be advantageous to first examine some of your teaching practices and see if changes can be made. However, sometimes there are children who continue to misbehave, regardless of what is going on in the classroom. The information in Table 4.1 may offer new ideas for handling certain off-task behaviors.

Table 4.1: Ideas for Handling Off-Task Behaviors

Problem	Possible Solutions
The student does not understand what is being taught or expected of him/her.	1. Establish a signal to clue the student regarding the off-task behavior and to determine whether he/she undestands your expectations. 2. Frequently in the lesson, ask the entire class to show a visual signal to demonstrate that they either understand, sort of understand, or don't understand. (For example, a thumbs up, sideways, or down displayed under the chin for privacy.) 3. Give feedback to the student.
The student does not think he/she can do the level of work required.	1. Decide whether the work is too hard. 2. Give some review. 3. Make any accommodations you can. 4. Give feedback to the student.
The student is acting out to get attention.	1. Give no attention to minor offenses. 2. Redirect with minimum of interaction or redirection. 3. Give positive feedback when the student is on task.
The student is acting out for some other reason.	1. Look for some other reasons to explain why the student is acting out. 2. Find time to discuss the reasons with the student. 3. Give positive feedback for correct behavior. 4. In a positive way, redirect the student back to the class rules. 5. Consider a behavior contract (discussed in Chapter 6).

Working With Centers in the Classroom

Centers can be an excellent way to motivate students and reinforce skills already taught. They can be used to provide interesting activities for those students who finish their work early, as a tutor-like activity for those who did not understand a lesson, or as an extension tool for students who can take the topic further. Some teachers use them regularly so that students can explore content at their own pace. Centers often allow the teacher to meet with small groups in order to differentiate instruction. Centers provide a nonintimidating environment that also focuses on specific areas of study. Although the management and establishment of centers-based activities can take a lot of organization and preparation on the teacher's part, in the end they can prove to be very effective. As always, it is important to clearly state directions and establish expectations. Lack of these will cause student frustration, confusion, and probably misbehavior (Wong & Wong, 1998).

Appropriate Use of Centers

Centers, or independent activities, can be used at any time of the day and for any content area. One specific option that works well includes having students work at centers during reading group rotations. While the teacher leads a reading group, the remaining students participate in centers. Some teachers integrate a "Must Do" list of centers to visit and then "May Do" centers that follow. If a teaching assistant is available during this time, he/she can assist students at centers or provide students with individualized instruction as needed.

There are many activities that are not possible in centers. Some independent activities will cause more confusion and chaos than learning. Because of this, there are certain things you will want to keep in mind when setting up and using centers. Centers need to be located away from the main flow of traffic, but also in places where teacher supervision and monitoring are easily managed (Marzano, Marzano, & Pickering, 2003). First, a center must reinforce a skill that has already been taught. Unless you have an adult or responsible student who can devote time to explaining the activity, children need to be able to do it successfully with minimal directions. For this reason, some teachers will only introduce one new center each week. Then the teacher can offer instruction, and the students will encounter only one new task while also returning to review tasks that they are used to in the other centers.

Watch to see if the children seem to enjoy each center. Since this is an independent activity, they might have a hard time completing a center activity that is not fun or informative. Next, watch to see if the center activities are too easy or too complicated. If so, they will create more problems than they solve. Do not be too concerned if every center does not work right away. Instead, take the time to adjust or change centers as needed. Also, monitor each center activity to see if it can be managed without creating a big mess. The teacher should regularly reflect on the grade-level appropriateness of a center or whether students are bored with having had the center for too long throughout the school year.

Finally, the teacher should plan for some form of accountability from each center. This accountability needs to be easy and fast for the teacher to correct or collect, but enough that the student feels the responsibility of accomplishing the task at hand. Determine which center activities can be completed individually, with a partner, or with the whole group involved at that center. Then, make sure expectations and procedures for each center are taught, explained, and posted. During center time, the teacher needs an established procedure for quickly dealing with students who lose their centers privileges, and what they will then work on without taking too much time from the small group or child whom the teacher is working with at that time. Furthermore, center time typically should relate to the content area of instruction. For example, many administrators have policies against math centers during the designated literacy block. Usually, teachers have more success in using just a few centers at a time. It is crucial to remember that centers are only to be used as an extension of what is already being taught by the teacher.

Sample Literacy Centers

Any content area can be reinforced using centers, and many teachers find them to be especially successful with language arts, where they can emphasize and reinforce concepts in reading, writing, and spelling. Some activities students can perform at independent centers are to read independently, record their voices reading aloud, or write letters or notes. Students may also spend their time publishing their own writing, possibly researching nonfiction books for a report, or reading and discussing a book with a small group of other students.

A simple literacy center activity I can try is ______________________________

____

____

____

The accountability I will require of students in this activity is ______________

____

____

____

Sample Math Centers

Math is also an area that lends itself well to center activities. The students can participate in math games, explore manipulatives to connect concrete thinking with the abstract concepts they are studying, or measure various items. The teacher could set a place for them to invent math questions, construct geometric shapes, or create a visual math problem. Calculator use is also very appropriate in a center if students are given instructions and tasks to accomplish. You might also want to ask the students to prove math concepts with manipulatives, make predictions, or create a chart. Use what you feel will reinforce the concepts your class is studying. Math centers should review recent concepts studied, allow ample opportunities to practice learned skills, or concretely reinforce the latest abstract concepts.

A simple math center activity I can try is ______________________________

____

____

____

The accountability I will require of students in this activity is ______________

____

____

____

Sample Science Centers

Science centers can be very interesting for many students. The teacher could consider using *Eyewitness* books on various topics, and then ask the students to investigate and report on the subject presented. They may also want to use a microscope to investigate simple objects, such as paper, feathers, sponges, or lace. With preparation and established management, the teacher could allow students to conduct a weekly experiment in which they measure and illustrate the results. Class science journals could also be included in centers to record observations, record properties of rocks or leaves, or find out how to use a balance scale to compare various objects. Determine creative ways to connect science with language arts by asking the students to read and report on biographies of famous scientists.

A simple science center activity I can try is ______________________________

____

____

____

The accountability I will require of students in this activity is ______________

____

____

____

Sample Computer Centers

Computer centers are perhaps one of the most popular types of independent activities teachers can set up. While you need to monitor anyone using Internet access, you can still use a computer as a great learning tool. You might want to have your class create an ongoing story or write a class newsletter. Older students might be assigned to read online newspapers and report their findings. There are many sites that allow your students to do interactive math problems, or perhaps you might want them to create their own problems using a drawing program. Consider how many computers are in the class and how you will guarantee equal computer access and sufficient time to complete any computer projects assigned. Consider having your students conduct research on the Internet. Perhaps you will want them to find information and report back to the group regarding an author, illustrator, or famous person in history. Many teachers also have their own math software to reinforce previously taught concepts. Students also love to write creatively using a word processing program.

A simple computer center activity I can try is ______________________

____

____

____

The accountability I will require of students in this activity is ____________

____

____

____

Reducing Transition Time

Transition time is the time it takes to change from one activity to another. The students may be changing from teacher-led time to group work or independent tasks. They may be moving from one center to another center. They may be moving from one content block of time to another content block. Every student also transitions as they enter or leave a classroom. Without rules and procedures, transitions can cause chaos that takes away from learning (Marzano, Marzano, & Pickering, 2003). Transition time is a common time for behavior problems, especially if the proper procedures are not taught, established, practiced, and frequently enforced. For example, if you tell the class to put away their writing journals and get out their math books, a certain amount of time will be spent doing this. This happens many times during the day and, after a while, this wasted time starts to add up. A teacher's goal in establishing procedures should be to work with the class in limiting transition time, because this is time during which no instruction is occurring. Teachers often find it difficult to reduce transition time. Here are some methods to shorten typical transition times:

- Before any transition time, first get the students' attention with a signal and state your expectations. Have them point to where they are going or visualize how they will get to the next activity. Then give a preestablished signal when they can actually begin to transition.
- You can tell your class they have only 20 seconds to prepare for your next instructional activity. Sometimes counting down backwards in a calm voice helps students regulate their responses and evaluate how much time they have to accomplish a task.

- If students are away from their desks working on activities, tell them to clean up and return to their seats. Once they are there, continue with your instructions. Step-by-step directions are often much easier to understand and remember.
- When students are transitioning into the room, always have something for them to do immediately. They should know automatically what to begin. Students don't always handle surprises well, and the younger the students, the more you need to prepare them. If anything in the room has been changed at all, let them know.
- If you want to have some fun while working on your transitions time, then turn it into a speed contest between different tables, boys versus girls, or the two sides of the room. Very young students often use chants or songs during transition time, with the expectation that everyone will be in the right place at the end of the chant or song.
- Give a warning or signal that transition time is about to begin. This can be a five-second warning or simply a bell that tells them to freeze and wait for your instructions. It is worth the effort to rehearse transitions, working to beat the previous time.

The transitioning technique I am going to try is ______________________________

____

____

____

This chapter has explored various strategies for engaging students in their learning processes. In order to be effective in this area, teachers must consider a variety of strategies in order to understand their content areas, understand the students in the classroom, evaluate the different components involved in the learning process, establish the available techniques and resources for teaching the content, and analyze and reflect on effective and ineffective teaching practices (Darling-Hammond, 1998). As closure, researchers Jana Echevarria, Mary Ellen Vogt, and Deborah Short (2004), in their observation protocol (the SIOP Model, which is devised mainly for teachers teaching sheltered instruction), call on teachers to critically evaluate the following: (1) the time allocated for each topic of study and the planned activities during that time; (2) the engaged time that students are actively participating in instruction during that time; and (3) the amount of academic learning time that students are actually focusing on the instructional content for which they will be ultimately accountable. If a teacher can improve student engagement in these areas, the teacher will no doubt see great increases in student interest, motivation to participate and, eventually, academic success.

Chapter 4 Reflection

1. How can you alter instructional strategies or assessment to better align with learners' various learning modalities?

2. How would you be able to incorporate grade-level appropriate centers into your classroom?

3. Evaluate your classroom on transition time. How can you improve this situation to increase instructional teaching time and engaged student learning time?

4. Evaluate the degree of student engagement in your classroom. What percentage of students is engaged at any given time? How many activities do you have planned that allow for all students to be simultaneously engaged in content throughout an entire period of time? Describe some of them.

Don't Let Everyday Problems Get in Your Way

Many teachers enter the teaching profession with ideal visions of standing before students and introducing important information into their lives. However, the typical school day extends beyond giving instruction. Even with the most disciplined classes, problems can and do arise, often during less-structured time periods, like recess or breaks. Often, the problems that arise are low-level misbehavior, such as students being noisy and rude. Even though the majority of the misbehaviors may be minor with occasional actual defiance, they interfere with teaching and learning, thus contributing greatly to teacher stress and burnout (Allen, 1996). In many schools, disagreements spiral into violent attacks. Students argue, threaten, and harass one another. Conflicts between differing racial and ethnic groups are also on the rise. Traditional scolding and suspensions do not appear to improve such situations (Eby, Herrell, & Jordan, 2005). In fact, research shows that the typical response of waiting for misbehavior and then punishing it is much less successful at changing and controlling behavior problems than planning for prevention of discipline problems and creating more productive learning environments in schools on the whole (Gushee, 1984). Because of this, it is important to instruct your students as to how to be peacemakers themselves so problems do not escalate to extreme levels. As this chapter guides teachers through various aspects of student conduct, it is important to remember that research does not show teachers one perfect way to deal with these problems; rather, teachers must be guided by practical, moral, and legal considerations as they decide what is best in creating their learning environments (Gushee, 1984).

Student Responsibility in Resolving Conflict

Before focusing on how teachers can react to common student misbehavior, teachers may want to consider preventative measures, such as teaching students how to resolve conflicts by themselves. Focusing on conflict resolution in the classroom links students to the concepts of democracy, citizenship, contributing toward a more peaceful world, cooperative learning, multicultural experiences, reducing personal prejudice, social justice, finding alternatives to violence, and using critical thinking to solve problems (Girard, 1995). Many teachers continue to use a reactive approach to discipline, having no idea what will set off their students the next time. Rather than thinking through what might be causing this behavior, they react impulsively. It is a challenging test of personal character when a teacher must deal evenly and thoughtfully with tense situations when they happen (Fischer, 2004).

With the right strategies in place, teachers can eliminate these overwhelming occasions. The secret to this is to teach your students to solve their own problems. One benefit is that students can then employ strategies to solve problems and avoid traditional disciplinary measures. Many teachers find ways to connect procedural instructions with conflict resolution instruction (Girard, 1995). This process has the added benefit of saving instructional time. When disputes arise, the students learn to address the problems themselves without coming to the teacher each time.

To take the responsibility away from the teacher and simplify the whole process, students need to learn the following three sentences:

- "I didn't like it when you . . . ."
- "It made me feel . . . ."
- "Next time I would like you to . . . ."

The wording can be changed for older students without changing the overall message. The teacher models these phrases early in the school year and offers the students many opportunities to practice and role-play. The teacher may need to post these sentences in the room for the students to use. After the students have learned them, they can practice using the process on their own. The teacher should try to be present for a confrontation or within visible sight of the students involved. If the conversation is going astray, the teacher can be ready to step in and take it back to the same three statements. When the dispute is over, ask each student if he/she is satisfied. If one student still feels the conflict is not resolved, then they start again with the teacher there to keep them focused. Some teachers employ peer mediation, where a third student is given the opportunity to help two students resolve a conflict (Girard, 1995). In addition, the teacher can keep a conflict resolution notebook in the back of the classroom where students can report successes and challenges while engaging in the procedure. This process keeps the problem solving short, focused, and shows the students how to accept responsibility for their own actions.

Five Primary Causes of Misbehavior

It is generally believed that there are five primary causes of misbehavior. Teachers need to think through how they would handle each kind of misbehavior. When they recognize and plan for them, many student problems can be eliminated. Above all, the teacher should strive to know the backgrounds, personalities, and driving forces for each student, in addition to any unusual family issues that might ignite a situation once the student is in school (Fischer, 2004). The types of students who tend to cause behavioral problems are students who are aggressive, resistant to work, distractible, or dependent on help (Wong & Wong, 1998). These students exhibit some form of behavior that differs from what is expected in the classroom ("Behavioral Disorders," 1993). Some of the causes of behavioral problems and ideas for helping this change of behavior are further discussed in the following sections. In any particular case, the teacher needs to identify what he/she wants the student to do and then consider how to redirect the current undesired behavior into the desired one ("Behavioral Disorders").

Boredom

Of the five, boredom is a common excuse that students give for acting out in the classroom. All students feel bored at one time or another. Even in the most engaging lessons, it can be a challenge to have the attention of every single student. The teacher needs to examine commonly used teaching strategies and instructional practices. Try using manipulatives in your lessons or changing teaching strategies every ten minutes. If the class is engaged in a group activity, break up the students further into pairs to share what they are learning with their partners before sharing with the entire class. Instead of always writing their answers on paper, allow the students to use small whiteboards. This addresses the needs of your more kinesthetic learners. Many teachers use simple games to teach a concept. For example, using cards with words that students put in alphabetical order can be more engaging than simply completing another activity sheet. Have related centers activities already set up for those who finish early. There is also nothing wrong with stopping and taking a break and continuing again after you have gotten the students' attention. A well-planned, engaging learning environment will motivate many of your typically bored students to participate and keep up with new and exciting activities in your classroom. Any time you try a new teaching strategy, such as sharing in pairs or on whiteboards, establish expected behavior or you will find that different causes of misbehavior may arise.

In the following sentences, list the behavior common of a student who exhibits this misbehavior. Summarize a simple plan for addressing his/her needs.

In my class, this student ______________________________

____

My plan for helping this student to overcome boredom is to ______________

____

____

Need for Attention

The desire to be recognized is a basic human need and something teachers cannot ignore. Every person wants attention and will sometimes go to great lengths to get it. In students, this desire for attention can even be subconsciously sought. How can you satisfy this need when you have a lesson to give? Try giving quiet students more attention. That will show others how to get the teacher's positive attention. For students who love the spotlight, give them tasks that require them to be in front of the class or a group of students. If you have students who constantly want to tell you something or ask irrelevant questions, you could give them five tongue depressors. They will owe you one each time they have something to share with you, but once their sticks are gone, they will have to wait until the next day. Another strategy is to tell these students to keep a dialogue journal that you can later read. To address both interpersonal and intrapersonal students, plan cooperative projects in which you assign the appropriate tasks to meet each of their divergent needs.

In the following sentences, list the behavior common of a student who exhibits this misbehavior. Summarize a simple plan for addressing his/her needs.

In my class, this student ____

____

My plan for helping this student to overcome the need for attention is ______

____

____

Power

Power is especially important to children who feel their lives are seriously out of balance. When this happens, they may try to balance the scale by controlling what goes on around them in the classroom. There is not much you can do to change their home surroundings, but there are steps you can take that can minimize the impact at school. Since this child may be used to hearing people argue, teachers can start by discussing a policy of refusing to argue out an issue in the classroom. Sometimes, your best position is to negotiate. This works very well as long as you limit the choices. For example, you can say, "If you would rather do this assignment at recess, that's okay with me."

Some children get power by being passive-aggressive. With this type of display for power, it may be possible to create a plan in which the teacher chooses in which areas to give choices and which areas are nonnegotiable. Sometimes the teacher can create a student area of choice that still accomplishes the teacher's academic intent for that student. Nelson, Lott, and Glenn (2000) suggest redirecting this need for power by asking for this child to help with something when his/her work is completed. Whatever plan you decide on, remember that students who struggle for power in the classroom need encouragement and validation just like everyone else.

In the following sentences, list the behavior common of a student who exhibits this misbehavior. Summarize a simple plan for addressing his/her needs.

In my class, this student ______________________________

____

My plan for helping this student to overcome the need for power is ________

____

____

Revenge

There are things in life that are self-defeating, and revenge is one of them. Children who constantly demonstrate revengeful behavior often feel like they don't belong. These might be the students who are constantly complaining about classroom rules not being fair. They might hurt other people in an effort to bring them to destructive behavior as well. Some of their violent behaviors are unhealthy attempts to identify their own feelings and their desires to have those feelings acknowledged by the teacher. The best thing to do is to build trust with reflective listening. A supportive conversation could begin with the teacher identifying and validating underlying feelings by saying, "I can see you are hurting right now. Tell me about it." You will want to help these students to discover how they can utilize their strengths and explain to them what their revengeful behavior will cost them. You may also want to teach through stories and other examples that revenge generally only escalates problems.

In the following sentences, list the behavior common of a student who exhibits this misbehavior. Summarize a simple plan for addressing his/her needs.

In my class, this student ____

____

My plan for helping this student to overcome revengeful behavior is ________

____

____

Self-Confidence

This problem extends to two extremes—too much self-confidence or not enough. For those who feel completely inadequate, you will need to teach them that even if they can't do everything perfectly, they can at least try different things. Often, these students assume the role of the helpless one, and others will notice and constantly come to their aide. To break this cycle, break down tasks into small steps, give no criticism while they are working on something, and encourage every positive step forward. Do not pity or mother them; instead, set up opportunities for their success. If you refuse to give in to their helplessness, they will in time find something they enjoy and can be good at. The teacher can try pairing them with others who can offer occasional help. Put these students in win-win situations whenever possible. For students who have too much confidence, foster their desire for autonomy by giving them challenging learning activities.

In the following sentences, list the behavior common of a student who exhibits this misbehavior. Summarize a simple plan for addressing his/her needs.

In my class, this student ____

____

My plan for helping this student to overcome issues with self-confidence is

____

____

Physical Needs That Get in the Way

Sometimes, students' needs are much more basic than those discussed above. Students' needs might be physical instead of emotional. Physical necessities cannot be calmed by nice words or smiles. They require action.

Hunger

The Seattle Times reported official statistics that show that 12.7 percent (or 37 million) of the population in the United States lived in poverty in 2004, while 11.9 percent of households (comprising 38.2 million people, including 13.9 million children) experienced food insecurity (Chelala, 2006). Obviously, the very real problem of hunger is going to affect student behavior and the ability to learn. It is vital for schools to plan for a program to feed them. If students do not have proper nutrition, then they cannot concentrate. In school programs where free meals are provided, sometimes the qualifying students do not take part because they feel ashamed. Often, the connection between food and energy may not seem obvious. Most children do not realize the causal relationship between what they eat and how well they can participate in an activity. To bring awareness to this problem, teach your students what nutritious snacks are and how they provide the fuel for the body's functions. Draw connections between sick feelings they have had or decreased energy levels after eating mainly unhealthy choices. Identify foods as "fun snacks" or "healthy snacks." Only allow the healthy alternatives in class and encourage students to limit the number of fun snacks they have at recess or lunch time. The teacher can model and reinforce the connection between diet and health.

Thirst

This is a physical problem, although teachers are sometimes irritated by what might seem to be an escape tactic by students. Thus said, thirst needs to be taken care of at the appropriate time. When you establish your class procedures, some teachers set up a maximum number of students who can get a drink during class, as long as it is not during direct instruction. Other teachers choose times when the whole class walks to get water. If you pick up your students at the end of recess, you can walk the line past the drinking fountain. To monitor turns, the students can count to three while the person in front of them is getting a drink. As a preventative measure, some teachers also allow the students to bring water bottles to class. Generally, the teacher should insist on cool, not frozen, water because the melting ice makes a mess. Some teachers allow trips to the drinking fountain in exchange for privilege tickets or recess time. This gives the students the power to make their own decisions. The teacher should educate the students and their parents about the importance of drinking water to quench thirst, rather than other sugar-filled or empty calorie juices and sodas.

Fear of Pain

Serious problems stem from both threats of physical and emotional pain. Bullying has been identified as a serious problem in many schools and communities. It can lead to serious emotional consequences for both the victim and the bully, but teachers do not always see or recognize it (Hyman et al., 2006). When you suspect a problem, approach the bullied child privately and make an attempt to find out what the child is feeling. If you don't have time to talk, ask the child to draw or write about the problem and how he/she would like it solved. Sometimes victims are reluctant to report a bully situation for fear of retaliation. It is all right to allow the student to stay in the room for a portion of recess or leave a few minutes early at the end of the day with the permission of his/her parents and the administration. If you see this as a bigger problem with your students, make the classroom a safe place by spending time talking about how every person is important and necessary to the group. If this is a schoolwide problem, the administration might want to consider specific bully prevention programs or character development programs that allow for education and role-playing.

One teacher in an inner-city school had a serious problem with one introverted student who was constantly taunted by other children for being different. After this child ran away from school early in the morning and was coaxed back by the principal, the teacher decided to give a whole-group demonstration on how bullying can affect someone. She brought in a perfect juicy tomato and talked about how beautiful it was. Then she poked it with a skewer on one side, explaining that someone made fun of the tomato. She discussed how no one could see the damage by that one poke, so another person came and taunted, poking another part of the beautiful tomato. She continued to poke the tomato, showing the effects of multiple taunting as the tomato deflated and the juices outpoured and there was hardly any tomato left. When she made this connection to students who are bullied, the classroom was silent. It made for a powerful visual that was referred to for the entire year by both the teacher and the students in the classroom.

Need for a Restroom Break

Restroom breaks can sometimes be disruptive and problematic. However, simple classroom procedural instruction are extremely helpful. Students should be encouraged to use the restroom when they are not engaged in class lessons. Remind older students to go to the restroom during their breaks and after PE. Young children will need to be reminded to go at the beginning of recess before running out to play. Most teachers discuss with students what to do when they feel that they really need a trip to the bathroom during instructional time. To minimize distraction during instruction, some teachers teach the students to use the sign language for restroom, one finger over the next. Other teachers let the students take responsibility for the lost instructional minutes by allowing them to go as the need arises but charging them five minutes during recess or after school. This way they are in charge and must take the responsibility to make the decision themselves. Students who continually cannot wait for breaks may have a medical problem. The teacher may wish to confer with the school nurse or with parents.

Space and the Physical Setup of the Classroom

If you live in a space for long enough, you can forget its obvious limitations. Your classroom itself may be part of a general management problem. Enter your classroom and look at it as if this was the first time you have ever been in the room. Initial impressions are made in the first 30 seconds. What do you see immediately? Take notes of the places where students may not have a good view of you or where it might be difficult for you to reach the materials you need. Another tactic is to sit in each student's seat and take notes on potential problems from that perspective. By doing this, you can critically reevaluate your space and what you have done with it. Ask someone else to give you his/her honest first impressions. When the room is full of students, look to see how well traffic flows. If you need more space, the easiest way to create it is to eliminate something from the room. Even if you think you might need it later, decide what is more important—room to roam or room to store. In many urban year-round schools, teachers have to rove from classroom to classroom each month. These teachers will want to discuss strategies with other teachers who have this experience in order to maximize storage while working in other people's classrooms. They need to make sure the administration supports schoolwide policies that aid in the instruction of the students in those rooms.

Break From the Predictable

Anything can become stressful and boring when you do it for too long. Sometimes, the need for change is so acute that it almost becomes a physical requirement. This is especially true for students with ADHD, or even the mostly kinesthetic learners. To keep the mind and body engaged, consider variations in your approach and the length of time you lecture. Sometimes all it takes is a two-minute stretch break to get you and your students back on track. You can put students in small groups and ask them to come up with a question for the class about what they have been learning. Or do stretches similar to what athletes do before a race. The teacher may consider changing the teaching strategy from auditory to visual or from visual to kinesthetic. Often, adding a well-structured listening and speaking activity about the content is all it takes. The benefit is that the students continue to reinforce the content while fulfilling the physical need to break from the traditional lecture structure. Perhaps you can assign your students to draw for five minutes to illustrate what they have been learning. For a lesson extension, they can present their illustrations to someone else, a small group, or the entire class.

Other Things That Can Get to You

Even the best of teachers can experience aggravation with the same old problems. Perhaps this is your case and you don't know what more you can do. Special problems require well-thought-out remedies and prevention strategies. Think about your teaching situation when you read about these commonly reoccurring student behaviors below. As you meditate on your plan for each situation, it is very important to also consider how you will devise opportunities for students to practice the new desired behaviors ("Behavioral Disorders," 1993).

Tattling

Students usually tattle on others in order to raise their own social station in the class. It is meant to hurt and put down someone else so the tattler can feel superior. When discussing this problem with students, the teacher should clearly differentiate tattling from telling the teacher of a potentially unsafe situation. There are different approaches you may use to solve this irksome problem. One method that works well with younger students is to make a "tattletail" out of yarn and paper and hang it on the wall. After clearly discussing with the students how tattling makes others feel and how it wastes learning time, the teacher can silently point to the tattletail each time someone starts to tattle. Some teachers invest the time to make small tattletails with each person's name on it. Tattlers have to give it to you if they want to tattle and they can only tattle once a day (or once a week). You might just decide to compliment the child on observation skills and tell him/her to come back at the end of the day with three positive things that person did. Another way to ensure that tattling is cut back is to require that tattling be given to you in writing. Some teachers keep a tattling journal available. Teachers should be mindful of their own practices as well; teachers often ask the tattler in the class to tell him/her what happened, which reinforces to that student that the teacher values tattling. Finally, you can use the conflict management system covered earlier (pages 108–110) and ask if he/she would like to talk to the other person about it.

My idea for dealing with tattling is ______________________________

____

Swearing

Schools must reinforce the time-honored principles of honesty, respect, responsibility, civility, caring, courage, and self-discipline. Many of these character qualities include a person controlling the use of swear words. The use of profanity is sometimes just an opportunity to feel mature, but these words can inflame an already tense situation. Some younger students do not understand why they cannot use words often used at home. It is vital for a teacher to calmly explain to the whole class the difference between school talk, street talk, and home talk. Some teachers set up a distinction between appropriate "private talk" and "public talk". Once the teacher has established the expectation that swearing is not appropriate in the classroom, the teacher will need to establish consequences for when a student swears. This is a problem in which it might be beneficial to include the class in deciding what could be a logical consequence. Perhaps the teacher will want to assign a paragraph in which the student can explain why he/she thought that cursing was necessary in that situation. Another possibility is to give access to a box where a child can write a word and slip it in if he/she feels an urge to swear. For some students who have become accustomed to hearing profanity at home, constant reinforcement will be needed. The teacher might have more success approaching this student as an ally, trying to help him/her rid himself/herself of a bad habit that could inhibit his/her goals for success in the future.

My idea for dealing with swearing is ______________________________

____

Note Writing

This is usually harmless unless it takes a person away from learning or contains a negative statement about someone else. The best course of action is to not read the note, but instead respect students' privacy. In order to avoid wasting a lot of instructional time to figure out who wrote a note and for whom it is was intended, the teacher might just want to tuck it into a designated place, reminding students that if they feel it is important, they can pick it up at the end of the school day. If this doesn't help, you might want to separate note-passing students or send notes home for parent signatures. If this is a big problem in your class, then it is highly possible that the classroom activities planned are not engaging enough or that sufficient lesson accountability is not required of students. Once these are in place, the teacher can take any found notes and direct students back to their learning activities or learning projects. You need to ask good, solid questions throughout a lesson that includes different teaching strategies. During times when lecture is necessary, plan for opportunities during which you pose a question, allow time for students to think of an answer and perhaps discuss it with partners, and then randomly call on students to give out answers. This strategy engages more students and gives less time to write notes, because they know they are going to be held accountable for giving a response to a peer or the teacher.

My idea for dealing with note writing is ________________________________

____

Pencil Sharpening

This seemingly small act can really disrupt a quiet classroom. To quiet the situation, you might want to have a cup of sharpened pencils and one with pencils that need to be sharpened, so that students may trade pencils instead of sharpening their own. You can assign students the job of sharpening pencils before leaving class in preparation for the coming day. Many teachers have a monitor who does this job during recess. If you prefer, you might want to ask if anyone has a sharpened pencil the student may use. Another simple way to handle this is to allow sharpening for two minutes in the beginning of class or insist that students use their own small pencil sharpeners. You will want to ask them to only use sharpeners that catch all the shavings so they don't fall on the floor.

My idea for dealing with pencil sharpening is ____________________________

____

Name-Calling

Most adults can remember specific names that they endured as children, whether the negative names related to their real names or their appearances. In some cases, this concern can be overcome by counseling the offending student. Students who often call others names are sometimes frustrated without knowing how to properly express emotions. Many times, these students harbor low self-esteem. The students involved should be encouraged to utilize the three communication statements on page 109 of this book.

My idea for dealing with name-calling is ______________________________

____

Chronic Lying and Stealing

Honesty is something you should be able to expect in a classroom. However, it can be very difficult to establish this expectation for all students. It is difficult to tell for certain if one of your students is lying or stealing unless you have evidence. Many times, students resort to lying in order to alter a version of the truth for their benefit or as a desperate attempt at protecting themselves. Another common reason people lie is to make their lives seem "better" or more interesting. This sort of lying can be a sign of low self-esteem, problems at home, or depression. Chronic lying can signal a psychiatric or social disorder and, as the teacher, you will need to believe very little of what these students say until they have a history of telling the truth. Once you have evidence that demonstrates a student told lies, meet with him/her privately and discuss an active plan in which he/she can win back your trust.

Stealing, for some, is a simple lack of boundaries. If you suspect that someone has stolen from you or from another student, take the time to sift through evidence. You might need to get witnesses together and listen to their versions. You should interview students privately and separately. Listen critically and rephrase what you think happened. Once you have evidence and collaborating witnesses, you can speak privately with the child accused. Sometimes it is effective to help the student return the item privately with an apology to the offended. The ability to help a child get out of a stealing habit is more important than simply getting back a five-cent eraser. Make sure you plan whole-group discussions on valuing others and their things and then plan for private continuation of that topic with offending students.

Stealing and lying are very difficult habits to stop. In order to break one of these habits, you may have to enlist the help of the student's parents or guardians. Set up a policy where the student is in charge of his/her behavior. If there is a report of him/her lying or stealing, take away something, such as his/her regular seat in the class or a special privilege. The child has to earn it back by going for one week without another incident. If he/she does lie or steal again, something else should be taken away. If it is a problem of stealing food, there may be other issues at work here, and you may have to discuss this with your administrator.

My idea for dealing with lying and stealing is ________________________________

____

Fighting

Fighting is something that boys, in particular, feel is natural, or even fun. Often, they do not see the seriousness of it because they love to clown around with their friends. Explain early on that you do not know the difference between play fighting and real fighting, so you treat them both the same. To handle this problem, you could ask the class to come up with other alternatives to fighting. If some damage is ever done in a fight, have the offending party correct the problem, e.g., holding the ice on the bump, mending a torn shirt with a needle and thread or even masking tape, or cleaning up any mess that occurred. Sometimes fighting happens between best friends. If this is the case, you can put them both on restriction from one another for one week. On the other hand, if they are not friends, you could require that they work together on a project for two days.

If it is a reoccurring offense with one child attacking multiple students, the teacher needs to involve administrators and parents in order to come up with appropriate actions. The student may need to stay with you or another adult during break time or be posted at an assigned place. If the fighting only occurs after school, you might want to dismiss the child later than everyone else. It is always a good idea to include the parents in any long-lasting interventions, in particular those that relate to after-school time. The parents and the teacher need to share responsibility for a cooperative working relationship that will work toward that child's learning and development (Clark, 1999). Sometimes, the parents can prove valuable assets as they share what they have already tried with particular behavior problems at home.

My idea for dealing with fighting is ______________________________

____

Playing With Objects During Class Time

This problem can be very simple to resolve. Explain that anything with which a student is found playing is considered a toy. Most schools have a policy against bringing toys, games, and other items from home. As the teacher, you can decide if you will return all confiscated items after school or if you will keep them until a parent comes to claim them. Some teachers require a signed note from parents to claim items. If a student plays with a confiscated item again, repeat your policy. Soon the parent and child will get tired of this and the item may not be brought to school anymore. If the item the student is caught playing with is something he/she needs, like lunch money, you can take it away and return it at lunchtime.

My idea for dealing with students who play with objects during class time is

____

____

Hopefully this portion of the book has helped you to formulate your plan for solving many of the tedious problems in the classroom that interfere with dynamic learning time. Another method for getting students more involved in problem solving is allowing them to analyze problems and establish solutions. Page 129 shows "The Problem Solver" form, which can work especially well with tattlers, chronic complainers, and introverted students who are too shy to talk to you about their problems. If a teacher desires to use it, the format and procedure for using it should be taught to the students early in the school year. The teacher can have a designated place where students can find the form. The teacher should explicitly explain what students do with the form after it is filled out.

The Problem Solver

Student's Name: ____

Today's Date: ________________

Tell about your problem: ______________________________________

Draw a picture to illustrate the problem:

How would you solve the problem? ______________________________

____

____

Can you think of a different solution to the problem? ______________

____

____

Describe what will happen once the problem is solved. ____________

____

____

Six Guidelines for Handling Common Misbehaviors

Structure—Structure—Structure

If you are having serious interruptions in your class, you are going to need well-thought-out structure. The more you are able to create and maintain structure in your classroom, the fewer potential problems you will have. You should make preventative plans of action for common problems (Fischer, 2004). This way, when they happen, you will notice them and be able to take care of them immediately. Structure doesn't mean rigidity. Rather, a structured approach is one in which students know exactly what is expected of them, which behaviors are acceptable or unacceptable, what the consequences are for each behavior, and what the time frame is for each expected behavior. Many teachers find that their most difficult students crave routine because it might be lacking otherwise in their lives. Once students are familiar with your routine, the problems will only arise when changes are made to that routine. This gives a well-planned teacher much more control in his/her overall classroom management.

Negotiate

Consider negotiating with a struggling student. This is often an unwelcome word to teachers, but it can really work with certain students. When there is a problem, everyone wants to feel a measure of validation and control, including the students. Give them guidelines and then let them choose what to do. Sometimes you may need to adjust some of your expectations and negotiate with students to reach common understandings, such as when and how assignments need to be done. When students have the opportunity to express their voices in classroom processes, they share in decision making and the construction of knowledge being learned

(Kordalewski, 1999). Always calmly discuss which areas, such as content required by standards, are nonnegotiable. Leave your own emotional concerns out of the discussion and never humiliate the students. As an example, when a student has been in a heated exchange with the teacher, the teacher can give an option, "Are you going to be able to solve this problem now or would you like to wait a few minutes?" Some teachers will allow certain students the freedom to walk to the back of the classroom if they need a moment to calm their unstable emotions before continuing to their desks to work.

You can often diffuse potentially difficult situations by allowing students to save face. This is always ideal if it means that the students get back to work quickly and without interfering with the learning process of others. Sometimes, certain students need to have a cooling-off period. Don't worry about a few minutes being lost when it allows everyone to get back on track without wasting the entire period. Giving some control to students in the learning process and the procedural routine of the class can deter problems. In addition, it can validate their active roles in their own learning journeys (Kordalewski, 1999).

Deal With Problems Quickly

Another thing to keep in mind is to deal with problems quickly, using as few words as possible. It is imperative to deal with problems promptly, with minimal instruction time lost (Wong & Wong, 1998). Train your students to recognize one word as a code. Saying "focus" is a quick way to tell a child to stop daydreaming and get to work. Some teachers will create a classroom mantra, and the students will know that if the teacher points silently to it, they are to read it silently, reflect on the class commitment to that word, and resume their work. If a student has a reoccurring problem, remember that you can make a running tally on the board or privately in a designated place so only he/she can see exactly how many times this problem occurs. Read more in Chapter 6 about individual behavior contracts.

Use Direct Language

It is best to use direct language when resolving problems. Tell your students exactly what you want, using specific mention of the behavior you want to see or the behavior you do not want to see. Don't rely on "knock that off" or "cut that out." It's better to say, "Put your sharpener away and read the chapter." Also remember to put a positive focus on directives whenever you can. Finish up by saying, "You are important to us," or "I value your education and I want you to learn what you need to know."

Know Your Bottom Line

All teachers need to know where they draw the line between working with a student and deciding that the student has misbehaved enough. The teacher should be aware of school policy and have a plan for when to send a student to another teacher's classroom, when to call the parents, when to send a student to the principal, or even when to call the police. Remember, a bottom line is just that. It is for serious offenses. Teachers should never threaten these actions unless they are ready and willing to follow through.

Follow Up

Finally, follow up on the problem. Once a crisis has passed, make a point of talking to the offending student during the day. If possible, express something positive but make a connection, even if it is neutral. With every problem, it is important to keep a log. This will help a teacher if problems involve more parties in the future. Figure 5.1 shows a sample log that teachers could use to document problems throughout the year. If the problem is very serious, make sure the administration knows what happened and what you did. When calling the child's parents, remember to keep your voice as nonconfrontational as possible. Start out with something like, "I wanted to let you know about an incident that happened at school today." If you and the parent come up with any future plans for the student, it is important to continue to communicate any further developments, positive or negative. Honest and frequent communication between teachers and parents helps ensure that there are no big surprises later in the year (Clark, 1999).

When teachers are dealing with problems in the classroom, it is very important to keep a record of what problems have arisen, which solutions the teacher has tried, and whether they have worked. If a problem escalates, the teacher has documentation to show how each step was managed along the way. This could prove very useful for teachers if parents do not want to believe a teacher over their child or if the administration has to step in where a teacher left off in the discipline of a student. The teacher can keep a small disciplinary record binder. Each page in the binder is designated for each student. The teacher should also keep any written correspondence from the student or parents, as well as copies of anything given or sent to the administration, to the student, or to the parents from the teacher.

Figure 5.1: Documenting Problems

Student's Name	Class	Date	Action of Student	Response by Teacher	Witnesses/Others Involved

Every teacher knows that teaching is more than just delivering content to students. While extra effort may be required for certain high-needs students, the proper management techniques needed for these students can increase success in overall classroom management (Marzano, Marzano, & Pickering, 2003). Teachers try to do their job while constantly navigating a classroom of varying emotions, changing attitudes, background circumstances, and problematic incidents. When teachers can anticipate common problems and create plans to resolve them, then they will be able to focus more attention on the task of actually teaching the students. The following chapter explores what to do when misbehavior problems escalate beyond the more straightforward solutions discussed in this chapter.

Chapter 5 Reflection

1. Which problems mentioned in Chapter 5 are the most common in your classroom?

____

____

____

2. What are some of the solutions that have worked in your classroom in the past for these common problems?

____

____

____

3. Reflect on your practice of including parents in the management and discipline of students in your classroom. List the reasons why this might be important and beneficial.

____

____

____

4. Write down the areas related to solutions for common misbehavior in which you want to seek out more ideas from colleagues in the near future.

____

____

____

____

Students With Behavior Needs

Teachers are sometimes called upon to work beyond the regular classroom curriculum and basic management systems when students enter their classrooms with significantly different needs. These can be students whose needs are not met by the standard curriculum or who do not benefit from the regular classroom set of rules and established consequences. While Chapter 5 looked at typical behavior patterns seen in classrooms, sometimes students enter the classroom with considerable behavioral problems that demand more in-depth and carefully-planned teacher concentration. Many schools have varying sets of procedures and support for dealing with these increased challenges. Sometimes, a teacher will have a lot of school site support and, other times, the teacher will need to work independently and resourcefully to create a positive working environment in the classroom. This chapter is meant to explore the many variables in behavior challenges that are presented to teachers. All students require creative yet caring plans in order to come up with behavioral solutions that allow them access to the curriculum in a constructive learning atmosphere.

General Principles of Crisis Intervention

A teacher often needs to address behavioral problems that extend beyond the regular established set of rules and consequences. There are students with tremendous behavior problems which can be trying on a teacher's patience and emotional state. Sometimes, these behavioral problems repeatedly interrupt the flow of instruction for the entire class. As a teacher strives to maintain a well-managed classroom, all students need to be encouraged to develop responsibility for their own actions. As students learn their content knowledge and skills from their teacher, there is also a need for them to learn knowledge and skills pertaining to conflict resolution, communication, and cooperative problem solving (Girard, 1995). Any well-established classroom management program should also include instruction in life skills that will create well-socialized students who learn how to be accountable for their actions. Students who are learning about logical and natural consequences will desire to behave in positive ways. The teacher of students with high behavior needs may need to take a deep breath at the beginning of each day and visualize a plan for dealing with the possible upcoming problems of the day. The teacher will want to find out just how much support the school administration and surrounding teachers are willing to give. Often, it helps to request an administrator or counselor to come and observe a student in question to help make a plan for how much intervention and support might be needed. One teacher recalls asking a district psychologist to observe a particularly angry student whose behavior was highly disruptive. The psychologist came in and the student was happily engaged in the morning lesson. The psychologist praised the teacher for using effective strategies for keeping the student on task. Frustrated, the teacher simply requested a return visit after the lunch break. Sure enough, when the psychologist returned, she saw the more typical, disruptive behavior and how the teacher's efforts were not working. Thus, the psychologist was able to help the teacher meet with a team of people to make a more effective instructional plan for the student. All of these actions need to be documented and parents should be involved in any plan of action for helping a student with high behavioral needs.

Early Intervention

Teachers need to catch potentially explosive situations as soon as possible. Look for clues such as a student's tone of voice and body language. If an outburst is prevented early on, there is a much better chance of limiting any further escalation of the student's behavior. One way of doing this is to move closer so that students feel less pressure to resolve a potentially explosive problem themselves. Sometimes, a teacher can back down in order to allow a student to redeem some of his/her perceived loss of power in a given potential confrontation. Students may need the option of finding a quiet place in the classroom to calm themselves down before returning to a lesson. Marzano notes that isolation and time out allowances only work if the student clearly understands why it is being allowed and if the teacher is not using it simply to get rid of the behavioral problem child (Marzano, Marzano, & Pickering, 2003). The teacher then can choose a calmer or less public time to revisit an issue with a student. The teacher's calm demeanor will always be helpful if a student has anger and power behavioral issues.

Communication

When communicating with a student whose behavior is escalating, the teacher should keep his/her voice flat and nonthreatening. It is generally favorable to use the student's name and talk only about the one behavior at hand. While using a clear, direct, and realistic choice, the teacher can simply tell the student what behavior is wanted rather than focusing on what he/she is doing wrong. This is not the time for a power struggle. If a student wants to argue, the teacher should repeat something like, "Nevertheless, I want you to. . ." until the student complies.

Body Language

When dealing with panic, rage, or irrational demands, teachers need to use every means at their disposal. Body language is the most important tool, followed by the tone of voice. The words teachers say are often the least important component. It is important for teachers to maintain a look of self-confidence and relaxation with their arms either at their sides or behind their backs. A teacher can turn so that he/she is facing the student at a 45-degree angle and move slowly, if at all. Since proximity can be intimidating, it is best for teachers to maintain a distance of about three feet from the student. Finally, the teacher should get between the student and the problem while looking him/her straight in the eyes.

Individual Work and Behavior Contracts

When a student often displays behavioral or work-habit problems, one effective strategy is to set up a daily contract with that student in order to alter behavior (California Teachers Association, 1999). With any established contract, the teacher needs to meet privately with the student to discuss the problem and why the teacher feels a contract will help. The contract should include clear definitions of the expected behavior, positive consequences for choosing to display it, negative consequences for not meeting the expected behavior, how any adults involved will offer support, and a plan for maintaining the desired behavior (CTA, 1999). The teacher should approach the student as an ally who wants to help the student avoid getting into more trouble in the future. In this role, the teacher should collaborate with the student to discuss the conditions of the daily contract. Parental involvement, with signatures and phone calls, is vital. The parents need to be involved in approving the contract so that they can reinforce it at home. The teacher, parents, and student should also discuss what happens if a daily parent signature is required and the student does not show the contract to the parent. The teacher might want to consider a section of the contract that shows improvement in case the student has problems in the beginning of the day. Then, this student will have something to work toward, rather than just knowing that the contract will be negative that day and therefore have no reason to change negative behavior for the rest of the day. Page 142 shows a sample daily contract.

The sample form on page 143 shows how teachers can support students with needs for developing good work habits by meeting with them at the beginning of the week to establish goals and then helping the students evaluate whether goals are being met throughout the week. Parental involvement is also highly beneficial in this process.

Sample Daily Contract

Student's Name: ____________________

Class: ____________________

Date: ____________________

	Yes	No	Notes
Redirections during the day			
Turned in all homework			
Finished all classwork			
Successful day at recess			

When ________________ earns ______ positive contracts, this will happen:

____

When ________________ earns ______ negative contracts this will happen:

____

Teacher's Signature: ____________________

Parent's Signature: ____________________

Student's Signature: ____________________

Daily Work Goals for the Week

Student's Name: ____________________________ Week of: ______________

	Language Arts	Math	Social Studies	Science	Other	Comments
Monday						
Tuesday						
Wednesday						
Thursday						
Friday						

When ________ earns _______ positive contracts, this will happen: __________

____

When ________ earns _______ negative contracts this will happen: __________

____

Teacher's Signature: ____

Parent's Signature: ____

Student's Signature: ____

Figure 6.1 shows a sample log that helps a teacher to account for rules broken. The teacher can use this log to document what has happened and then record the appropriate consequences he/she applied. This can be kept with the classroom behavior and discipline binder documentation system discussed in Chapter 5.

Figure 6.1: Behavior Log

Behavior Log for ________________________________

Date: ___________ Time: ___________ Location: _______________

Check Those That Apply

_______ fighting
_______ chewing gum
_______ talking at the wrong time
_______ arguing
_______ disrespectful
_______ out of seat
_______ making noises
_______ pouting

Consequence applied: ____

Teacher's Signature: ________________________________

Parent's Signature: ________________________________

Student's Signature: ________________________________

Similar to the behavior contract, some teachers establish a work contract that can help a student to learn responsibility in staying on task and completing assignments. The teacher, student, and parents should work together to discuss why the contract is needed, which components will be included, how it will be evaluated, and what consequences and rewards will be set up at home and at school. Figure 6.2 shows a sample.

Figure 6.2: Work Contract

Student's Name: ______________________________ Date: ________________

Subject	Assignments	Due	Completed	Comments

Any assignments not checked off and signed by the teacher are to be completed at home and returned by the due date.

Teacher's Signature: ____

Parent's Signature: ____

Student's Signature: ____

An incident may occur when a student or a teacher moves beyond an acceptable line. It is very important to keep record of all problematic incidents. Figure 6.3 demonstrates a simple way to document incidents.

Figure 6.3: Incident Documentation

Date: ______________ Time: ___________ Place: __________________________

Persons Involved: ____

Description of Incident: ____

____

Witnesses: ____

Interventions Taken: ____

Parent and/or Administrative Signature: ______________________________

Challenging Scenarios

To meet the diverse needs of all students, teachers need to be prepared with multiple options. If a teacher's first reaction in a difficult situation doesn't work, he/she can and must adapt quickly with a new response. Studying and discussing challenging scenarios with another teacher can promote the development of classroom management skills

Thus far, this chapter has discussed many of the problems that interfere with the teaching process. Following are examples of challenging scenarios to give teachers practice and application in promoting critical thinking and problem-solving skills in the classroom. Each case is followed by possible solutions that will prompt teachers to analyze the situation and formulate a plan of action to address the problem.

For each scenario, once you have chosen what steps you might take, write down your own thoughts for handling the problems.

Scenario 1: You have a student who constantly interrupts the lesson by speaking out, making noises, or bothering someone around him/her. Mark the choices you would try.

- ❑ Explain that you respond to those who behave correctly and then stick to it. After that, totally ignore students who want your attention but don't want to follow your rules.
- ❑ Divide the class into groups and give points and rewards to each group for good behavior.
- ❑ Post your consequences for not following the rules.
- ❑ Move closer to this student.
- ❑ Carry around a clipboard and look as if you are writing down the student's name when he/she is acting out.
- ❑ Plan for questioning strategies in which you ask a question, have students think silently, share answers with a partner or group, and then pick sticks from a can to designate who will respond to the question before moving on.

What else could you try? ____

____

____

Scenario 2: You have a student who never finishes work on time and you know he/she understands how to do it. You are frustrated. Mark the choices you would try.

- ❑ Try giving a time limit to do a short portion of the assignment.
- ❑ Give a reward for work finished on time.
- ❑ Sometimes the child wants control, so try to get buy-in by asking how much he/she thinks can be done in a certain period of time.
- ❑ Challenge the student by making it a contest.
- ❑ Seek help from other teachers who may know this student.
- ❑ Give time warnings (e.g., "We have ten minutes left. . .").
- ❑ Be positive. Tell the student that you understand that more time is needed and that he/she will get that time during recess.
- ❑ Plan a work habit contract with this student.

What else could you try? ____

____

____

Scenario 3: This student simply won't follow directions. Either he/she is not paying attention or did not hear the directions correctly, but you know you will have to repeat every direction just for this student. Mark the choices you would try.

- ❑ Make sure the students know exactly what you expect.
- ❑ Ask all students to repeat directions to a partner, one at a time.
- ❑ Stand near this student when giving directions.
- ❑ Check to see if he/she understands the assignment before getting to work.
- ❑ Assign a peer buddy whom the student can ask instead of always coming to you.
- ❑ Start your directions with that student's name.
- ❑ Create a signal that students (or possibly the one student) will use to indicate that they understand your directions.
- ❑ Walk around and check students' work. If you see any problems, work privately with them.
- ❑ Assign peer tutors who can work with others who have questions.

What else could you try? ____

____

____

Scenario 4: The students in your class just seem to refuse to be quiet, to pay attention, or be cooperative. You haven't had this problem before and aren't quite sure why it's happening now. Mark the choices you would try.

- ❑ Explain again exactly what your standards are.
- ❑ Move around the room. You own the portion of the room that you possess.
- ❑ Call attention to students who are working effectively.
- ❑ When dealing with a problem, do it quietly and privately.
- ❑ Develop and practice a signal for getting students' attention.
- ❑ Make a contest between the different parts of the classroom. The winner gets to leave the class on time. The others wait for one minute to strategize how to win the next time.

What else could you try? ______________________________

____

____

Scenario 5: Transitions between activities in your class take about three minutes. You have been told that that is entirely too long but you haven't been able to improve. Mark the choices you would try.

- ❑ Tell the students what you expect them to do and how long you want it to take.
- ❑ Time the transitions or ask different students to time the transitions each day.
- ❑ Make it a game where students compete with one another.
- ❑ Rehearse transitions.
- ❑ Prepare yourself for transitions as much as possible by having everything ready.
- ❑ Pass out supplies and have directions written on the board whenever possible.
- ❑ Keep students focused by shortening the assignment periods. If you need to, allow time to finish the assignment later. Once they get off track, transitions become that much more difficult.
- ❑ Teach a signal to get students' attention and then use it.

What else could you try? ______________________________

____

____

Scenario 6: When you start talking, the class doesn't recognize that you want their attention. They just don't clue into the sound of your voice or recognize that it means something special. Mark the choices you would try.

- ❑ Speak in a low tone so that if you do raise your voice the contrast will be noticed right away.
- ❑ Create a signal that will alert students that you want their attention, such as clapping three times, turning the lights off and on, ringing a bell, putting your thumbs up where students mimic you, or counting from five to one.
- ❑ Stand and wait.

What else could you try? ____

____

____

Scenario 7: One or several of your students use profanity and put-downs. This is hurting the morale of the entire class. Mark the choices you would try.

❑ Explain your rules to the class immediately.

❑ If necessary, allow the class to practice using these three phrases: "I don't like it when you. . ."; "It makes me feel. . ."; and "Next time I want you to. . ."

❑ Speak privately to the student and explain the consequences of doing this again.

❑ Ask the student if he/she knows what the swear words mean (be prepared in case he/she does).

❑ Hold a class meeting on appropriate words and inappropriate words to use in the classroom. Make a class contract and have everyone sign it.

❑ While you listen, have the student call home and explain to his/her parent what was just said.

What else could you try? ______________________________________

____

____

Scenario 8: Fights, threats, weapons, and drugs are becoming more prevalent on school campuses everywhere. Even though we understand that these problems exist, most teachers don't expect to encounter them and are often unprepared when or if it happens. Mark the choices you would try.

- ❏ If you come upon a fight, send for help from either another teacher or an administrator.
- ❏ If you can determine who the victimized student is, tell him/her to go to the office.
- ❏ If weapons of any kind are found, refer the child to the administrator.
- ❏ Prepare ahead of time to find out what constitutes a weapon.
- ❏ Learn the signs of drug abuse in a student or parent.
- ❏ Dismiss threatened students early, with parental and administrative permission.
- ❏ Call for a conference with parents.

What else could you try? ____

____

____

Scenario 9: Sexual harassment comes in many forms. Sometimes it is only an off-hand remark from a young student that is inappropriate. In the most extreme cases, it becomes sexual assault. Mark the choices you would try.

- ❑ Talk to the students involved, including witnesses, as soon as possible.
- ❑ If you determine that this is a small first-time offense, or that the person involved didn't understand, handle it yourself.
- ❑ If there is a pattern of behavior, refer the case to the principal or vice principal.
- ❑ Find out more about the personal history of the offending student.
- ❑ Contact parents or legal guardians.

What else could you try? ______________________________

____

____

The purpose of this portion of the chapter has been to help you think ahead so you can react with confidence in an unexpected situation. The case method, which has been used for many years to educate business, law, and medical students, works just as well with teachers. It gives you a useful means to explore challenging scenarios that you have already encountered in your career.

It is inevitable that you have had challenging scenarios in your teaching career because it is the nature of children to test the limits. In the broad scheme of things, this is a good thing because it ultimately helps them develop the skills necessary to be successful in a complex society. Of course, that doesn't help you maintain discipline in your classroom.

You have seen that there is no one perfect answer to situations that can occur in the education environment. Teachers want to be sure to build trusting relationships with students, plan cooperatively with other teachers and support personnel in their schools, develop appropriate goals, maintain personal accountability, and reaffirm their commitment to all student success (Sanacore, 1997). Overall effective strategies include a sensitivity to students' needs and interests, as well as flexibility in helping students learn.

Chapter 6 Reflection

1. What are some of the most challenging situations you have found yourself in as a teacher? What did you try and was it effective? Why or why not?

2. What adjustments can be made in your classroom management plan to accommodate students with considerable behavioral needs in your classroom?

3. How can the inclusion of behavior or work contracts benefit students in your classroom?

4. Why is it so important to document all behavioral incidents and events in your classroom? List specific examples.

Students With Special Needs

Teachers are often called upon to work with students with special needs, including in general classroom settings. Many children with special learning needs do not get their needs met because the standard curriculum is not modified or is inappropriate for these children. Frustrations and off-task behaviors in students with special needs arise because their needs are not being appropriately met. Often, children with special learning needs do not have behavioral challenges when the curriculum is modified. In addition, there are children who have behavior issues and need curriculum modifications and alternative behavioral interventions. Thus, it becomes necessary for a teacher to fully investigate what needs a student has and the reasoning behind any behaviors that a child may be exhibiting. While this chapter will discuss a teacher's responsibility to meet student needs, it is certainly not advocating that teachers diagnose and treat these needs. However, a teacher will indeed need to analyze and probably modify current teaching delivery methods in order to meet special needs in the classroom.

Students With Disabilities or Special Needs

According to the Individuals with Disabilities Education Act (IDEA) of 1990, which was federally reauthorized and amended most recently in 2004, federal law ensures free appropriate education for students with disabilities, designed and suitable to their individualized needs and provided in their least restrictive environment (20 U.S.C. § 1416). A least restrictive environment means educating the child with disabilities to the maximum extent possible with typically developing peers (20 U.S.C. § 1400). The removal of these children into special classes or separate schooling occurs only when the nature or severity of the disability of the child is such that education in a regular class with the use of supplementary aides and services cannot be achieved satisfactorily (20 U.S.C. § 1412).

Once a student is identified and found to qualify for special services under various eligibility and disability standards that can differ by state, an Individual Educational Plan (IEP) is developed. A team of specialists, including special education teachers, general education teachers, school counselors and psychologists, administrators, and parents collaborates to set educational goals (20 U.S.C. § 1414). These professionals are excellent resources for the teacher. In order to meet the demands of federal law, teachers need to adjust their teaching practices and expectations.

Once an IEP is developed, the teacher is then required to meet the child's specific learning needs and is also accountable for monitoring and updating progress toward specified goals and objectives. If a child can work well in a general education classroom with the help of an IEP, pullout services, partial special day services, or aid of a resource specialist teacher, then that is what is designated. If the child needs to be in a separate class with a special education teacher, then that is what is provided. Usually, the placement is decided by the team of people already mentioned, and the range of appropriate student placement varies by state, district, and school-site designation. Public school teachers are expected to provide effective instruction for students who enter their classrooms with an IEP.

One of the main ways to individualize education for these special needs students is by modifying the curriculum and implementing methods established in the student's IEP. Partnering with parents is vital as well in this process. While teachers do spend a considerable amount of time with students, they do not see the children in a wide variety of environments. The parents can help the team of educators see the whole picture of the child in order to accurately format a plan to meet that child's needs. Once an IEP is in place, the teacher is then required to meet the child's specific learning needs and is also accountable for monitoring and updating progress. There is a wide spectrum represented among students who qualify as children with disabilities or special needs. The diagnosed student needs range in functional ability and severity from mild to moderate to severe. The IEP is designed to specify which needs will be met and by whom in the school setting.

However, some students in the classroom will not have an identified special need at all. The teacher may decide to have the school counselor or psychologist consult on whether the child qualifies for services or not. Every school site has its procedures for this, usually some type of student study team. By law, a child can only be referred for special services assessments after the resources of the regular education program have been utilized. This again involves an open discussion with parents, which can help a teacher accurately identify the behaviors that need to be addressed in the classroom. It is very important to remember that teachers and educators cannot diagnose students with special needs; they can describe and refer, but they cannot apply the labels themselves.

Sometimes, teachers assume that the frustrations experienced by students with special needs in their classroom are behavior issues. Children with special needs do not always have behavioral issues, although many do when they become frustrated and confused. As this chapter has explored, the actuality is that often these students' needs are not being met by the curriculum or by the teacher's appropriate accommodations and modifications. IDEA also specifically addresses that when discussing the discipline of students with disabilities, the disability must be taken into account (20 U.S.C. § 1415). The teacher needs to be aware if a behavioral intervention plan has been included with the IEP.

Every teacher of students with disabilities should be continually evaluating whether a particular behavior is related to the disability or to a lack of appropriate accommodations and modifications for that child to succeed in the least restrictive environment. Accommodations include extra time or changing the amount of work to be completed in a specified amount of time. Teachers do not change the basic lesson; rather, modifications refer to actual adjustments in lesson delivery or material covered. Many times, behavior problems arise if the child's needs are not being adequately met or if a child's special needs have not been correctly identified. Furthermore, the teacher needs to be sensitive to frustration levels with students with special needs, because a lower threshold for frustration may result in more outbursts or an easier tendency to want to give up (Echevarria, Vogt,

& Short, 2004). There are further regulations on some disciplinary methods, such as suspension limits for students with disabilities. Students with special needs may think and behave differently from other students when it comes to discipline.

Working With Students With Special Needs

Students with mild, moderate, and severe disabilities are increasingly being included in general education classrooms with the aid of IEPs, team teaching with special education teachers, and the inclusion of the appropriately trained aides and resource specialist teachers ("Including Students With Disabilities," 1993; Sanacore, 1997). In order for a student to succeed in the academic and behavioral realm, there is a great need for research-based strategies that teachers can employ, as well as research-supported behavioral ideas for helping these students do well. Many of the strategies will also prove helpful for the special education teachers who instruct students with special needs in a self-contained special education classroom.

Getting Students Started on a Task

Teachers of students with special needs should believe that these students can succeed, and they should be committed to accepting responsibility for the learning outcomes of these students ("Including Students With Disabilities," 1993). This commitment can be demonstrated in the extra effort exerted in helping these students attend to their schoolwork. The teacher should let the students know when they need to begin a task and how long they will have to complete the task. An overhead timer or other visual timer can be beneficial for the teacher and the child. Sometimes, an IEP will require that the student be allowed extra time for some or all tasks. If possible, the teacher should stay with these students until they finish their initial resistance stage (e.g., "I can't do this" or "Why do I have to do this, it's stupid?"). If the whole task is daunting for them, the teacher can ease their frustration by breaking the large task into smaller parts (e.g., "Put the title on the page." "Write your introductory sentence." "Cover everything except the first math problem.") The teacher should praise and reward these students' efforts promptly. It is effective to provide specific, prompt positive feedback, such as "Good job writing your title." The teacher should work to reduce the amount of visual information on the page if possible.

Helping Students Stay on Task

The teacher should clear away as many distractions as possible, especially on the students' desks. If necessary, some teachers turn the desk around so that the student won't have the distraction of grabbing things inside of it. General classroom clutter can be very distracting for students with special needs. It is helpful to use file folders by standing them up on the student's desk as study carrels. The teacher can additionally strive to reduce sources of background noise like air vents, street traffic, and playground noise (Ciocci, 2002). Some students benefit from headphones to block out noise. Sometimes, the students actually concentrate better with a rubber ball to hold—their tension goes directly into that object. The teacher should be aware of the extra time often needed for students with learning differences to process information (Echevarria, Vogt, & Short, 2004). The teacher can assign a neighbor to tap softly on their desks to remind special needs students to keep on task. A teacher can also employ a secret signal he/she has worked out with the students to remind them to get back on task when peer prompting is inappropriate for them. The teacher can reward on-task behavior by giving praise or a reward like a chip to be used later for a preferred activity.

Some students with special needs require specific methods for asking for help when confused, like holding up a colored card for the teacher to see. The teacher should encourage all of the students in the classroom to be socially engaged during cooperative group learning, which will further encourage them to help each other when needed during other parts of the school day ("Behavioral Disorders," 1993). The teacher also needs to consider visual presentation of material and pacing of questions during instructional lessons (Ciocci, 2002).

Guiding Students to Work Without Interruption

Depending on the special needs represented, the teacher should know what to expect. The teacher should learn about the students' needs from available support staff. The teacher should consider which behaviors to permit that do not disrupt too many other students and yet allow students with special needs to accomplish their own work successfully. Some students may feel a great need to get up and walk around for a little while. The teacher can use this as a reward after a set amount of time on task. Whenever possible, the teacher can let them stand and do their work. Some students benefit from a "sensory seat," an inflated cushion to sit on, which helps them stay in their seats. Another key suggestion is to keep them away from areas of distraction, such as the door, pencil sharpener, or drinking fountain.

Helping Students to Follow Directions

Teachers of students with special needs should have the skills to select and adapt their instructional methods in order to meet the needs of these students ("Behavioral Disorders," 1993). Students with special needs may not understand or register subtle hints. They cannot always process indirect language or comprehend the hidden classroom agenda, or rules, which other students may have internalized. The teacher must be direct and use as few words as possible. He/she also needs to carefully consider the use of figurative language. Students with special needs can be very literal. If a teacher tells a child to "spit it out" when he/she may mean to speak quickly, the child may actually start spitting. The teacher can intentionally plan instruction to teach students with special needs to process commonly used figurative phrases. Repetition and practice are critical (Echevarria, Vogt, & Short, 2004). The students with special needs can be asked to repeat and explain to partners what they are supposed to do. Some students can role-play the expected behavior.

New challenges arise when giving instruction in a classroom with students with special needs. On pages 167 and 168, there are some simple strategies that teachers can put into effect that will allow the instruction to be effective for the students with special needs and disabilities, without taking away from the instruction geared to all the students in the classroom. Not every modification will be helpful or necessary for every student with special needs.

Teacher Checklist of Classroom Modifications for Students With Special Needs

- ❑ Reduce the number of assignments or the number of problems to solve in a given assignment.
- ❑ Decrease the amount of writing for an assignment or allow for word processing.
- ❑ Modify the tests—for example, read math problems to the student, shorten spelling lists. This is usually an area designated on the IEP.
- ❑ Extend the time for assignment completion.
- ❑ Sign up the student for a homework center.
- ❑ Use a visual timer to determine the amount of time to be spent on a particular assignment.
- ❑ Use visual aids when giving instruction.
- ❑ Give short, concise directions.
- ❑ Have a buddy repeat the directions to the student.
- ❑ Allow the use of a personal chalkboard or whiteboard.
- ❑ Provide a special study area.
- ❑ Change the cooperative group.
- ❑ Provide a special learning partner.
- ❑ Have the student use a notebook/contract for organization.
- ❑ Request an organized desk area and notebook.
- ❑ Allow work time in another classroom if it will allow the student to work without distraction or solve a peer problem in the classroom.
- ❑ Provide "activity breaks."
- ❑ Have the student use a computer for writing assignments.
- ❑ Have the student dictate thoughts or a story to an aide. Use a small tape recorder, if necessary.

Teacher Checklist of Classroom Modifications for Students With Special Needs *(cont.)*

- ❑ Allow the student to copy the dictated story.
- ❑ Encourage the student to use a marker for tracking while reading.
- ❑ Change the student's seating. Reflect on whether the student needs to be closer to where you will be or farther away from distracting students.
- ❑ Put fewer problems on each page. Enlarge print.
- ❑ Assign short periods of concentrated effort.
- ❑ Shorten the student's assignments. Don't give out assignments that don't reinforce required content concepts.
- ❑ Provide the student with the opportunity to take the assignment home or to the homework center.
- ❑ Provide written directions.
- ❑ Ask the student to repeat your question before answering it. Utilize the strategy of having all the students share answers with a partner before they are accountable for answering the teacher.
- ❑ List assignments on the board and ask the students to copy them. Many children with visual-processing problems cannot copy from a board, so have them copy from another student's book or provide it already written to the student.
- ❑ Break complex directions into one or two step tasks.
- ❑ Change class assignments.
- ❑ Allow the student to use headphones to screen out distractions while involved in paper and pencil task.
- ❑ Put a hand on the student's arm or shoulder to gain and maintain attention for orally presented materials.
- ❑ Vary test format.

Working With Students With ADD/ADHD

At this time in education, there are 13 federal categories of disabilities. Attention Deficit Disorder (ADD) and Attention Deficit Hyperactivity Disorder (ADHD) are not recognized as federal disability categories for educational labels for IEPs. However, many of the strategies described in this chapter also work with students with ADD or ADHD. Students with ADD or ADHD can be some of the most lovable and yet difficult students with whom a teacher will ever work. It is important that teachers responsibly understand and accept the condition and the children. Students with ADD or ADHD need structure, redirection, and understanding. This syndrome, with set criteria designated by the American Psychiatric Association, is characterized by difficulties in attention span, impulse control, and sometimes hyperactivity. It often begins in infancy and continues to have a harmful effect on a person's ability to adjust at home and at school through adulthood ("Teaching Children With AD/HD," 1998).

Teachers of students with ADD or ADHD will have to provide a very well-managed environment for these children to function successfully. The rules will have to be clear, reasonable, and consistently enforced. Patience may be tried constantly, but teachers should keep faithful to the established program. Certain preventative accommodations and modifications will make the learning day easier and less prone to behavioral problems for the teacher and the students. First of all, the teacher should establish a classroom environment that provides consistent organization and clear procedures. Seating the student near the teacher, providing him/her with good student role models, and keeping him/her near the front of the seating arrangement with his/her back to the rest of the class often helps these students stay focused ("Teaching Children With AD/HD," 1998).

Giving students choices is good, but they should be limited during the day. The teacher will need to provide immediate and appropriate consequences, both positive and negative, and ignore as many minor disruptions as possible. The teacher should also provide immediate and brief verbal redirections and give immediate feedback on assignments. Research shows that students with ADD/ADHD work most positively when any special conditions offered to them, such as stimuli-reduced study areas, are also offered to the other students so that they are not made to feel "different" ("Teaching Children With AD/HD," 1998).

Sometimes, the ADD/ADHD student may need work that is specifically tailored to his/her ability. The teacher can accommodate the assignments to be less complex and, whenever necessary, broken down into smaller components. Along with this, the teacher can provide some way for this student to move around, as an outlet for hyperactivity. Daily homework accountability logs with teacher and parental signatures might be helpful, as well as daily notebooks for parental communication ("Teaching Children With AD/HD," 1998). The teacher should highlight this student's strengths, not just his/her weaknesses. Finally, it is crucial to remember that this is someone's child, and they love him/her very much.

Sometimes, teachers argue that they cannot treat one student differently from the rest of the students. They complain that unequal treatment is not fair to the others. They are reluctant to change their teaching practices for a particular student. However, federal and state law continually support the idea that equal treatment is not the same as equal opportunity. Educators need to allow students access to the appropriate curriculum. This means that teachers have to make allowances or change assignments for some students so that they have equal access to the required content concepts. This situation arises whether a student has special needs or even second language needs. The term "fair is not always equal" applies to students with disabilities and other special needs.

Chapter 7 Reflection

1. Does your responsibility to students with special needs in your classroom affect how you plan to establish your management and discipline plan?

2. What adjustments can be made in your classroom management plan to accommodate students with special needs in your classroom?

3. What accommodations can be put into place to help meet students' special needs?

4. What modifications can be put into place to help meet students' special needs?

Communicating and Working With Parents

The relationship between teachers and the parents of their students is vital in the overall education of students. Parents are the students' first and most influential instructors (Wong & Wong, 1998). Sometimes, working with parents can be a difficult job. The vast majority of parents are genuinely interested in the well-being of their child. However, even with this interest in mind, there can be differing views surrounding the issues of parental involvement in the education of their child, parental influence in how the classroom is managed, and parental agreement concerning the best ways to address any behavior matters. Good communication skills are important in any profession, but for the successful teacher, they are essential. Teachers can establish rapport with parents by using effective communication skills. These skills can enlist the help of parents in order to teach students to make responsible decisions and contribute to the overall goal of a positive learning environment. Nonetheless, the process of recruiting the support of parents can take a good deal of effort and time.

Usually, the initial impression a teacher gives goes a long way toward setting the tone for the school year. If the original contact is negative, that will negatively affect each time a teacher tries to work with the parents throughout the year. The early impression is established by the type of communication set by the teacher from the very beginning of the school year. Parents are an important part of the child's learning, and every teacher needs their help. Preventative measures will be advantageous. With the goal of seeking cooperation and support, parents need to receive a copy of the classroom management plan, detailing the consequences and rewards (Wong & Wong, 1998).

If a teacher talks to parents only when there is a problem, then that teacher is working with strangers, not partners. In relationship to discipline and classroom management, parental support from the beginning is an important component of the success of schoolwide conflict resolution management plans (Girard, 1995).

What Every Parent Believes

The very concept of human relationships is complicated. The relationships involved among the teacher, parents, and students are no different. It is in a teacher's best interests to enlist the parents as supporters and partners. "The evidence is consistent, positive, and convincing; families have a major influence on their children's achievement in school and through life" (Henderson & Mapp, 2002, p. 7). Teachers can usually assume that all parents love their children, but often this love can play out in different ways than the teacher expects. The goal is to try to understand the beliefs that parents hold about their children. If the teacher is aware of these beliefs, it can help create more effective communication as the parents and the teacher work together to help the students live up to their potentials.

Obviously, a parent has very specific ties of love to his/her child that a teacher will not have. Parents usually believe that their child is unique and special. They feel like they know their child better than a teacher could possibly know the student. While they may acknowledge that children, in general, may not always tell the truth, they might feel that they can believe anything their own child says. Parents often advocate for their child's rights; in fact, it is one of their fundamental parental duties (Clark, 1999). They see their role as the main defense between their child and a harmful world. Parents regularly think that they are acting in the best interest of their child. They may challenge a teacher's strategies because they believe their child can learn almost anything if it is presented in the correct way. A common aspect in the teacher and parent relationship might also be that any remarks on student behavior are seen as a judgment on their parenting ability. Some parents are very concerned with the reputations of their child; they may think that others remember every bad thing their child does and form opinions based on this.

Parents may not totally understand the school system. They enter a classroom with this apprehension about what they do not understand. They may fear that the school maintains a "permanent record" that determines what their sons or daughters can become in life. The room for misunderstanding grows even larger if the parents had little schooling when they were growing up, if they grew up in a different country, or if they speak a different language than the teacher. An example of cross-cultural miscommunication and misinterpretation given by researcher Ann-Marie Clark (1999) is that a teacher may say that a student is performing in an "outstanding" manner, but for some cultural backgrounds, it is considered a negative characteristic to stand out in such a manner. What the teacher means as positive may be interpreted disapprovingly by the parent.

With all this in mind, a teacher should listen carefully when a parent speaks, not only to the words but also to the underlying emotions and beliefs. Teachers need to remember the above points and validate the adult's love and ability to parent. Once parents understand that their child's teacher is not judging them, the teachers will be able to work together with them in the best interest of their child. As teachers build alliances with parents that validate their concerns and contributions, these connections directly relate to improvements in student achievement (Henderson & Mapp, 2002).

Ways of Communicating With Parents

Every teacher needs to have at least three different methods of communication. It is important that the first three communications in a school year with parents be positive. This will enable the parents to react in a much more receptive way when the teacher needs to call parents about negative behavior. Parent communication needs to be accessible. Therefore, translation is absolutely necessary if any parents speak a language other than English. In fact, by encouraging first-language use and maintaining a positive attitude toward second-language speakers, teachers not only create a welcoming climate for the second-language-speaking families, but also promote the children's pride in their linguistic talents and overall academic confidence (Cummins, 1991). The district should be able to help with this need if a teacher is not fluent in the languages represented.

The first step toward effective parental communication is to evaluate the types of communication that a teacher has in place. Then, the teacher needs to evaluate what each form of communication accomplishes for the parents. Finally, the teacher should reflect on whether further modes of communication are necessary. In Table 8.1, check the the techniques you already use. At the end of the list, be sure to include any other ways in which you commonly communicate with parents.

Table 8.1: Ideas for Communicating With Parents

- ❑ Phone call before school begins
- ❑ Ongoing phone calls
- ❑ Class newsletter
- ❑ Weekly or monthly calendar
- ❑ E-mail
- ❑ Notes
- ❑ Talk before or after school
- ❑ Conferences
- ❑ Home visits
- ❑ Class website
- ❑ Open house
- ❑ Report card
- ❑ Progress report
- ❑ Additional forms of communication:

As the teacher considers the most effective ways to communicate with parents, consider how often the parent is able to accomplish the tasks in Table 8.2 with the typical forms of communication already in place. Check those that apply.

Table 8.2: Ways Parents Can Assist Their Child

- ❏ Express expectations about their child's education
- ❏ Feel invited and welcome at the school
- ❏ Understand the child's progress in the classroom
- ❏ Share insight into student's home study styles
- ❏ Discuss the child's interests and behavior issues
- ❏ Understand what concepts the student is learning
- ❏ Understand how they can help the student learn more at school
- ❏ Understand their role in helping the student with homework
- ❏ Initiate contact with the teacher if they have questions or concerns
- ❏ Become involved in volunteering at the school
- ❏ Extend learning concepts through home activities
- ❏ Discuss future academic possibilities
- ❏ Understand the avenues for the child to reach certain academic goals, like college
- ❏ Understand the various levels of parental involvement available at a school

Adapted from a chart (Henderson & Mapp, 2002, p. 22)

When You Call Parents

When a teacher better understands what the parents believe about themselves and their child, the teacher can use that information to create successful communication when he/she calls the home. Most phone calls from teachers to parents are negative. Therefore, the teacher can break this cycle by making positive phone calls. If a call is for negative behavior, the teacher should keep the focus on the behavior, not the student. If the teacher has already sent a detailed account of the discipline plan, then the phone call home can serve as the teacher's request for the parents to take an active part of the action plan in order to improve the behavior, not the individual student (Wong & Wong, 1998).

Before calling parents, it is best to send a note ahead of time to let them know that you would like to talk about an incident at school. If you don't have the time to send a note home before calling, then start out the conversation with a comment such as: "We had an incident at school and I wanted to let you know about it." There is no reason to set up a negative atmosphere of panic or judgment, so make it clear that you are happy to invite them into a discussion of what is best for the student. Talk to all of the parties involved in an incident and write down any facts you may have, ahead of time, so you are sure of the details. It is really important that the parent sees you as a partner in solving problems, not as an adversary. Plan ahead of time how you will initiate the conversation (e.g., "I appreciate being able to talk to you," "Thank you for all of your help," or "You've done a wonderful job with Johnny.") Parents might not understand your expectations of their involvement in solving the problem. Therefore, it is important to be clear and tell them if you require their action or if you just want to keep them informed.

Take a deep breath and relax if you need to call a difficult parent. You are the parent's agent inside the classroom, and you are both working together for the child's good. Always be ready to provide ideas for solving a problem at school if the need arises. Never get into an argument with a parent. Always treat the parent as your equal. After this phone call, follow up on anything you said you would do. They will really appreciate it if you let them know when you see a situation improving. Choose one of the forms of communication on page 177 to update the parents on progress. Finally, always thank the parent and give him/her the credit for making the necessary changes.

Teachers deal with many students each day. Therefore, it can become very difficult to remember which issues arose for which students. Page 181 shows a sample communication log. This is helpful for documenting any communication you have with the parents of a student. If you have set up a management binder of documentation (first referred to in Chapter 5), then each completed log sheet should be entered behind the appropriate child's section in the binder.

Communication Log

Student's Name: ______________________________

Parents' Names: ______________________________

Home Phone: ______________ Work Phone: ______________

Family Information: ______________________________

____

Ongoing Issues: ______________________________

____

Health Issues: ______________________________

Date	Subject	Concerning	Response/Action	Follow-Up Information

Parent Conferences

Parent conferences can be intimidating for new and veteran teachers alike. Many times, teachers are afraid that parents will ask difficult questions or put them on the spot. The teacher needs to remember that it is okay to not know everything. The focus should be on working with parents to help their child succeed in school. Open and frequent communication reduces unhappy surprises at conferences, and both the parents and the teachers benefit from being well prepared to discuss what is best for the child in a trusting atmosphere based on respect, trust, and confidentiality (Clark, 1999).

Hopefully, the first communication with parents won't be the official parent conference. Parents are vital to a student's success, so get them involved early with invitations to the classroom, notes of praise, or other forms of communication. You may even want to send home a letter listing the points you will cover in the scheduled conference so that parents will be informed and prepared. As the teacher makes a schedule for parent conferences, flexibility is important. Parents' involvement is shaped by their perceptions of their own skills and abilities and their experiences with feeling welcome and invited to be involved at the school (Henderson & Mapp, 2002). The teacher may also need to schedule translators for parents who do not speak English. Speak to district personnel if this is a problem at the school site. When the school establishes a system where second language speaking families are also seen as partners, they will not be excluded from participation in the school setting because of their language, and they can be shown effective ways to help their child's learning process in spite of the language difference (Cummins, 1991).

Consider an agenda when you set up the meeting. It is best to start out sharing the student's positive qualities, as well as allowing some time for parents to share valuable information about the interests their child has at home and any concerns that they want to discuss in the conference. All parents love to hear nice things about their children. Be sure to show the student's work and discuss test scores, including previous year-end tests. If this is a time where you present the report card, explain what the grades mean. Behavior is an important issue, so you will want to discuss conduct and peer relationships. At this point you might want to ask parents to share further questions and concerns. Invite them to write a note listing their concerns if they think of further questions when they have returned home. This lets them know they are equal members on the team. Finally, wrap up the meeting and define goals for the coming months. This may include changing seats, altering class work, getting special help for the student, or establishing a time to do homework or a place to put it when finished.

Points to Remember

Educational jargon like "criterion-referenced testing," "learning modality," and "least restrictive environment" will not be understood by most parents. Avoid these education-specific terms and rephrase them in commonly understood terms. During routine parent conferences, it is unusual to run into parents who are abusive and hostile, but it can happen. Listen to the parent in as pleasant a manner as possible and tell yourself that this is not about you, it is about the child (or sometimes the parent). If the teacher is anticipating problems, perhaps an administrator can be asked to drop in during the scheduled conference.

When addressing specific learning problems, parents and teachers should work together. Both need to discuss the context of a problem so that they can pinpoint whether the child is experiencing problems with peers, family pressures, or specific subjects or learning situations (Clark, 1999). Parents can then be a great asset to the teacher by identifying what will help the student and in making a plan to address some of the problems surrounding the learning concerns with concrete changes at home, as well as supporting changes that the teacher will try in the school environment.

The Basics of Conferencing

Some generalizations can be made about conferences. Teachers generally become more comfortable with them as they gain more experience. It is helpful to make a conference schedule form and post it outside your door for parents to see as they arrive. Also, give a copy to the office and any other person who might need to be involved, such as a resource teacher, speech therapist, counselor, or translator. Organize the report card, student work, test scores, and other accompanying materials before you begin so that it helps keep you on track. It is also a good idea to have a pen, some paper, and post-its on the table for note taking. Be sure to schedule enough time for questions and discussion so that other parents are not kept waiting too long. It is wise to try to schedule difficult conferences at the end of the sessions to allow extra time to talk. However, if you need to keep the time short for any reason, then schedule another conference immediately after, in order to keep the general schedule moving along.

Even the most organized parents will sometimes forget an appointment. To make sure you aren't sitting around waiting, send out reminders one or two days ahead of time. This will help to ensure you talk to all the parents. If you can't get some parents to come in, consider phone conferences for these parents. Send the report cards home with the students and call the parents in the evenings to discuss them.

Start the conferences on time so parents are not kept waiting. Greet them at the door if possible and walk into the room with them. If you aren't sure of their names, ask by saying, "I'm sorry but I don't know your names." As you start, sit next to them in the same size chair. Keep the conversation focused on the child, even if the parents want to discuss their own needs or compare this child to a sibling.

Be prepared to discuss the important issues for each student. Look over the report card, test scores, and any other important information beforehand so that you can give accurate facts. It is okay to be honest about the student's strengths and weaknesses. Parents need honesty about any academic problems so that they are not surprised by consequences, such as hearing that a child is at risk for retention, further down the road. Use honest but sensitive phrasing. If the child is average, say that he/she is "right on track." For those children who are behind, tell parents that they are "struggling." Be specific about which subjects and activities need further support. Note in which areas the parents will need to provide further support and which areas of need will mostly be addressed in the school setting. If there are academic problems, it is important to give possible solutions. Parents need specific guidance in the areas in which they can help the child.

Know your grade-level expectations and have a good understanding of what is required at the grade level below and above your own. Take notes when necessary. If you and the parents develop a plan, be sure to write it down and specify which person is responsible for which helpful assistance. Demonstrate specific helpful activities, such as flashcards, and show parents how you teach difficult concepts so they can reinforce these at home.

It is a good idea to invite the child to be a part of the conference if he/she is mature enough. Many schools even ask older students to run the conference. This teaches them to take ownership in what they have accomplished. If you have another appointment and the parent keeps talking, stand up and hand them any forms you may have for them. Leave some open slots at the end of your conferencing period for parents who missed their appointments. You may also want to give yourself some free time during your schedule so you have a chance to relax. Otherwise, you may find yourself saying the same things over and over with little relevance to the child being discussed. If you are new to the process, it is best not to start out with a lot of conferences on the first day. Give yourself some time to get comfortable with the process.

Questions to Ask Parents During Conferences

It can be insightful to ask the parents what their child has to say about school or whether there are any particular thoughts about what the class is doing. Perhaps they have their own concern about their child's progress in school. You might ask what they and their child feel about the homework policy. Find out what some of the child's favorite or least favorite subjects in school are. This is also an excellent opportunity to find out if the child has any special needs that should be considered regarding his/her performance in school. Ask the parents if they understand the grading system. Allow them to share goals they have for the child or goals the child is already working toward. Finally, find out if there are any questions they would like to ask of you. It is very common for teachers to find parents who are primarily concerned with their child's behavior and other parents who are primarily concerned with their child's academic progress. Strive to create a balanced discussion of both issues in the conference.

The form on page 188 will guide you through your practice responses to questions that might arise during a parent conference. It is very important to maintain an informed professionalism and to be prepared for discussing the academic and behavioral issues surrounding each child in the classroom. Consider that sometimes parents' questions can have underlying confusion about the teacher's expectations in the classroom. The teacher needs to specifically clarify what is expected in order to help the child learn how to monitor his/her own ability to comply with these expectations (Clark, 1999). This form is helpful because sometimes parents don't know what is important to ask. The teacher can bring up the subjects about which the parent may not have known to ask. For practical application, pick out one child in your class or one child with whom you have worked and create answers to these potential parent questions. Remember, you want to be complimentary and yet as factual as you can be.

Page 189 contains a sample form that can organize the information that the teacher wants to cover in a parent conference. With a form like this, the teacher can check off the information covered, even as the parent's questions and concerns are addressed. The concept surrounding this form can easily be adapted for different grade levels. The teacher would want to make a similar form addressing the main concerns important to the content covered and academic goals for the specific child.

Sample Questions Parents Ask During Conferences

Student's Name: ______________________________ Class: ____________________

1. **How is my child doing?**

   ____

   ____

2. **What is my child's overall behavior like?**

   ____

   ____

3. **How does my child get along with others?**

   ____

   ____

4. **What is my child going to learn this year?**

   ____

   ____

5. **Is my child progressing as well as expected?**

   ____

6. **What are my child's notable strengths?**

   ____

7. **What do I need to do as the parent to help my child?**

   ____

Other questions I am often asked by parents:

____

____

Information Organizer for Conferences

Student's Name: ________________________________ Date: _________________

Thus far in this reporting period we have had ________ assignments, tests, and quizzes.

Your child's scores are:

______________________ ______________________

______________________ ______________________

______________________ ______________________

______________________ ______________________

______________________ ______________________

______________________ ______________________

Therefore, the overall current grade is: ____

This grade is not final and is subject to change depending on make-up work and/or future work. If this score is unsatisfactory, there is still sufficient time to bring it up to an acceptable level.

Teacher's comments: ____

____

____

Parent's comments: ____

____

____

Parent's signature: ____

Strategies for Successful Parent Conferences

Below are strategies for boosting your effectiveness when meeting with parents. Grade yourself on each point. Work on the areas that are your biggest challenges.

Area	Grade	Ways to Improve
Clarity I say exactly what I mean and check to be sure that I am understood.		
Professionalism I am friendly, yet businesslike. I never discuss others negatively or compare one child with another.		
Positive Attitude I build up the adult's ability to parent and the child's capability to learn.		
Documentation I plan ahead so that I have work samples to back up what I have said.		
Assertiveness I come across as being in charge of the meeting with clear ideas of how to improve any situation.		
Flexibility I am able to change my mind when corrected and able to come up with alternate plans.		
Inclusion Whenever possible, I include the child when I am discussing future plans that include him/her.		
Knowledge I understand my curriculum and am able to present it in layman's terms. I also know several strategies for working toward the student's future growth.		

Teachers cannot successfully reach all students effectively without some parental support. When schools and families work together to support a child's learning process, this child generally does better in school tasks, stays in school longer, and enjoys school more (Henderson & Mapp, 2002). As the teacher learns how to invite and incorporate parents into the classroom, he/she can reflect on the strategies that work best and the techniques that seem to have the most positive effect on the students. If learning and behavior problems are involved, children are most likely to succeed in solving these problems when teachers and parents, who have a mutual relationship of trust and respect, examine the context of any problems and work together to cooperatively formulate a plan of action (Clark, 1999). Henderson and Mapp (2002) give these further suggestions:

- Teachers should assume that all families can improve their child's school performance.
- Teachers need to actively help parents know how to guide their child's learning process.
- Teachers can work with families to help them become better connected to the school.
- Teachers can share ideas so that the school is better connected with families.
- Teachers need to demonstrate respectful and trusting relationships with parents.
- Teachers need to embrace an attitude of partnership in all of their communication with parents.

Chapter 8 Reflection

1. What are successful strategies you already have in place to strengthen the teacher-parent relationship?

2. In what areas can you further strengthen your effectiveness in your relationship with parents?

3. Evaluate your current use of the various ways to communicate with parents.

4. Choose one strategy in which you want to improve and describe how you think it will positively affect the learning process for your students.

Bringing In Help With Peer Consultation

Increased workloads and rapidly changing student needs result in an increased amount of stress for educators. Because of this, it is rare for a teacher to not require additional help at times. Just like everyone else, teachers make mistakes, try too hard, or come up short. Teachers are usually isolated within a classroom with minimal adult interaction through the majority of the day. This can seem unbearable when there are added classroom management troubles. Teachers do a disservice to the students and themselves if they don't occasionally ask for support. There is no way a teacher can know what to do in every situation. There is no individual teacher who can do it all, know it all, or make all the right decisions. There are times when teachers will need to reach out to other teachers as a resource.

One of the best and least intimidating ways to get support is through peer consultation. This is when one teacher asks another teacher to help with one or more confusing aspects of the day-to-day classroom teaching process. A teacher may consider this possibility when he/she is considering an area of teaching or class management where growth is desired. It can be a one-time request, but there are also many teachers who access ongoing personalized assistance and peer coaching from a consulting teacher. This is someone to talk to when there are general questions over a longer period of time. Perhaps a teacher desires to see modeled lessons by another teacher who has found an easier and more effective method of teaching.

Additionally, sometimes small groups of teachers will meet to plan units of study or a month of activities. These groups can also work together to discuss strategies for dealing with typical student problems. Often, teachers who are at the same grade level or teach the same subjects can participate in this kind of cooperation. This process of collaboration can decrease the feelings of isolation and the overwhelming need to get too much done. When it comes to teacher collaboration, administrative support varies by school, district, and state. Sometimes planning time is designated for minimum days with less instructional student time or as part of professional development-based staff meetings. Sometimes, principals offer roving substitutes and release time in order to cycle through various classrooms and offer pullout planning time for groups of teachers or observation time for sets of coaching partners. Attending a good professional development seminar can also be a great help. As a further support, many districts offer assistance from curriculum specialists. It is important for every teacher to seek out what assistance is available from their districts or school sites.

Mentoring and Peer Coaching

First of all, it is important to mention that each state, district, and even school site may have different programs in place, as well as requirements and terminology. These programs often refer to mentors, coaches, consultants, collaborators, or colleague support. Mentoring is assistance offered through districts and usually includes peer coaching. This type of help uses experienced teachers who support and assist both novice teachers and experienced teachers new to the district. Sometimes a district offers a formal mentorship period of one to two years. Many states now mandate new teacher coaching programs for all first- and second-year teachers. California's program Beginning Teacher Support and Assessment (BTSA) provides formative assessment, individualized support, and content-area collaboration in the form of experienced and trained coaches who help new teachers effectively transition into the teaching career (California BTSA, 2006).

New York requires a one-year mentoring program involvement for all new teachers with the initial certification as part of their compliance with the federal No Child Left Behind program (New York State Education Department, 2006). There is also the highly acclaimed new teacher support program called The New Teacher Project (2006), which has worked in over 150 school districts in 22 states to give students excellent educational experiences through highly qualified teachers. Programs such as these offer ongoing training for the coach teachers and many resources for the teachers being coached.

In addition, there are also programs for teachers who are not new teachers but who request to take part in coaching-funded programs. California has a program entitled Program Assistance and Review (PAR). Other states have programs in place, as well.

In peer coaching, teachers receive support, feedback, and assistance from fellow teachers. This leads to shared collaboration and commitment toward using effective teaching practices and improving learning for all students (Carr, Herman, & Harris, 2005). Carr, Herman, and Harris (2005) differentiate the terms *mentoring, coaching,* and *collaboration* in their book *Creating Dynamic Schools Through Mentoring, Coaching, and Collaboration.* Mentoring has the purpose of new teacher induction support by experienced teachers, using the methods of observation, feedback, and co-planning. Coaching matches all levels of experienced or new teachers for the purposes of instructional improvement and professionalism to work beyond the beginning support into how teachers can improve instruction, assessment, and instruction. With coaching, rather than just the new teacher gaining support, both teachers in the pairing receive and give mutual support. Collaboration can add the element of the administration working with teachers for the purpose of the organization of the school programs. Collaboration also results from teachers serving on committees and departmental teams or advisory councils in leadership roles for the purpose of planning instruction, assessment, and making recommendations for school-site issues.

The most common method usually involves (but is not limited to) teachers observing teachers. In *mirror coaching,* the coach records only that information in a particular area identified by the person being observed. After the observation, the coach turns any collected information over to the subject for the purpose of analysis, reflection, and change. That person does all the reflection and planning without further assistance. *Collaborative coaching* is identical to mirror coaching with one difference—the other teacher still collects only the data asked for, but will also meet with the observed teacher to go over the observation. The coach in this situation will guide self-reflection by asking questions which help the observed teacher to analyze whether or not the lesson objectives were met. Yet another method is *expert coaching,* in which a master teacher serves as the coach. The expert may be a mentor who works exclusively with a novice teacher or a teacher new to the district. The expert is free to collect any information he/she thinks is important. Afterwards, there will be a post-observation during which the mentor will guide the discussion. Any well-established model should stipulate that peer-coaching evaluations are confidential and not to be combined with administrative official evaluations as a part of a teacher's professional permanent file. Through cooperative efforts, all teachers can draw on more experienced teachers to help develop new skills.

There are many benefits when teachers participate in coaching and mentoring relationships. These benefits foster professional growth and development for all teachers involved in the process (Holloway, 2001). Well-implemented coaching programs offer a reduced sense of isolation, an ability to implement new teaching strategies effectively, and a revitalized sense of effectiveness. The best programs offer focus and structure. The most helpful models are supported by the administration with time allotted for planning, meeting, observing, and analysis. Effective coaching relationships can be aided by videotaping lessons, using dialogue journals and portfolios, participating in debriefing discussions, and utilizing teaching standards to measure successful teaching practices (Scherer, 1998). Many programs also offer training for the coaches. On the individual level, these programs can improve actual teaching practices, and on the school-wide level, these programs can lower the rate of teachers leaving the profession or school (Holloway, 2001). More benefits include strategically planned instructional time, higher levels of teacher reflection on their own teaching practices, and more emphasized goal setting for the academic success of students in the classroom.

Whom Should You Ask?

Whom should you ask to be your peer coach? This is a very important decision, and one that takes some thought. Teachers will usually find that there are various possibilities. According to author James B. Rowley (1999), a good mentor displays these six qualities: (1) commitment to the role of mentoring; (2) empathy and assistance when problems arise; (3) skill at providing instructional support; (4) adaptability to the context of the relationship with the teacher being mentored; (5) modeling continuous learning and professional growth; and (6) ability to communicate hope and optimism.

One opportunity may be to ask other teachers in the district who have been specifically trained to be peer coaches. The principal or district office should provide a listing if such help is available. Often teachers feel more comfortable with a respected teacher at the same grade level or a similar content area who is considered successful and effective. Certainly the chosen person should be one who treats others with respect and confidentiality. Perhaps you will decide to informally ask someone for assistance and support when needed. These collaborative relationships will take time, so commitment will be vital. Another option is for teachers in a particular grade level or subject area to pair off in teams for coaching opportunities.

It is normal to question and undermine yourself when you first think about getting help from someone else. These thoughts might include, "What will the other teacher think of me?" "What can I learn?" or "Will this be a bad reflection on me to my principal?" Initially, all teachers may consider similar fears concerning this process. However, the process of collaborating with colleagues should be seen as just another learning experience. Just as teachers do not require the students to come in knowing everything, neither should they expect the same of themselves and other teachers.

What Should You Expect From Peer Consultation?

The National Education Association's (NEA) guide for creating new teacher support systems outlines 13 jobs that mentors of all experiential levels can exemplify: supportive counselor, teacher, challenger toward personal best for all teachers, coach who helps teachers improve classroom environment, observer with ongoing coaching and support, facilitator through a broad range of educational experiences, trainer through workshops and professional development, master teacher, tour guide, advocate, role model, reporter who shares a fellow teacher's successes, and peer colleague (NEA, 1999).

Your tutoring process can best be broken down into three simple steps:

1. The first step is to take some time to meet with the peer coach. This should be a convenient time when both teachers can sit down and be honest and reflective. Perhaps the teachers can pick a set time each week. This needs to be a time when students are not in the room. During this time, they might open with concerns about teaching, management style, or perhaps recent evaluations. If trust and respect have been established, both teachers can be open.
2. Secondly, schedule observation time. Both teachers will benefit from observing each other. A more experienced teacher will better be able to help a new teacher if he/she has seen the newer teacher's practices in action. A less experienced teacher will learn a lot from seeing experience in motion. During the observation, the teachers might want to identify an area of need, possibly related to keeping the students on task, lesson pacing, transitions, or organizing a particular subject matter. Many times teachers find they need help handling difficult stu-

dents or something as seemingly simple as test taking. Whatever the questions, most veteran teachers have had to work through identical problem at some time, and they can offer support in these areas, once they see where support is necessary.

The biggest challenge in classroom observations is finding the time to do this when you are teaching yourself. Some suggestions are to ask for a half-day substitute teacher to watch the class (the substitute can change classrooms so that both teachers have a chance to observe the other), or do it during the prep period or differing breaks. Sometimes, an administrator can be asked to fill in for a short period. Some create this time by combining the two classes and trading teaching.

3. The third step in the process is to allow time for both teachers to analyze what was seen in the observation, discuss problem areas, reflect on needed changes, and make plans and goals for improvement. If an area of concentration has been chosen, this time can remain focused on that. It is best if the teachers can meet on the same day of the observation, but with some time for personal reflection and even note-taking before the discussion.

Peer coaching and mentoring will probably not solve all of your teaching problems at once. It is important to consider taking incremental steps toward becoming a more effective, reflective, and strategic teacher. Whether you are meeting as a group of colleagues working together for planning or as a pair of teachers, it is important to schedule more conference or observation time, if it is still needed.

Chapter 9 Reflection

1. How would it be helpful to you to have a peer coach?

2. In what areas of your overall teaching practices would you most desire support and feedback?

3. In what areas of your overall teaching practices do you feel you could offer support and feedback to others?

4. How do schoolwide peer-coaching programs benefit students overall?

Creating Your Own Classroom Discipline Plan

Thus far, the book has discussed reflecting on current classroom management practices, providing a positive learning environment, preparing for a system of rules, consequences and rewards, keeping students on task, and dealing with everyday problems. The book has also addressed specific needs, such as students with special needs, teacher actions for high needs behavioral issues, communicating with parents, and working with other teachers to improve overall teaching practices. Certainly by this time teachers should understand the high correlation between student behavior and academic progress and one's teaching practices and effective establishment of classroom management. The behavior that is exhibited in the classroom affects not only how the students see the teacher, but how administrators, colleagues, and parents view the teacher as well.

Discipline problems often affect the administrator's decisions whether to rehire teachers or award tenure. It is also the main source of career-related stress as reported by teachers, and the number one reason that former teachers reported they left the profession. As the book has established, success in this area, and indeed teaching as a whole, begins with a classroom discipline plan. It is important to now go through the process of establishing a successful plan to prepare teachers in creating a good working and learning environment. Although no such plan can anticipate and prepare for everything you might encounter, every teacher needs to begin somewhere.

An effective plan needs to be based on the students' and the teacher's genuine respect for one another and an understanding of one another's needs. Anticipation of appropriate behavior, responsible living, and individual autonomy creates an atmosphere in which rules are understood and followed. The teacher and the students alike should be able to acknowledge good decisions and positive actions. With a well-thought-out discipline plan, the teacher can reinforce and redefine expectations. Thinking through and setting the limits may be challenging, but it is a necessary step toward classroom control.

Different Models for Consideration

When preparing a discipline plan, the teacher should first consider what the objectives and options are. As you read through the following ideas, look for what you think will work for your class and your personality. Research does not point to one model that works for every teacher, student, and situation. Therefore, teachers need to evaluate different components and implications involved in choosing from the different models. Certainly, you need to try only those approaches that seem appropriate to your specific situation and your comfort level. Often it is useful to try new approaches, especially if what you are currently doing is not working.

There is no single proven way to manage every class and get every student to behave and stay on task. One of the reasons for this variance is wide diversity of local school policies relating to what teachers can and cannot do to discipline students, as well as what support teachers are given in management practices. Before you can start to outline your own plan, you have to know what your school or district will permit. Only then can you establish your own policy that will fit inside the school plan.

While you are designing what you want in your class, you should remember to put your effort toward reducing discipline problems, not toward eliminating them altogether. Regardless of what you may think, every teacher experiences discipline problems from time to time. If you start with an all-or-nothing mentality, you will probably fail. That is because students are unpredictable, and learning discipline is like anything else we teach them—it takes a lot of time and repetition.

Below, you will find a short synopsis of different methods for creating positive classroom management systems. They are summarized by Thomas H. Allen in *Developing a Discipline Plan For You* (1996). Look at them and decide which elements speak to you. If you feel that components from several of them might work, keep them in mind as you create your own plan.

The Ginott Model—Addressing Misbehavior With Modeling

Dr. Haim Ginott, a well-known author of effectively addressing children's needs and feelings, wrote the revolutionary books *Between Parent and Child*, which was written originally in 1965, and *Teacher and Child*, originally written in 1972. He felt that discipline is best taught in small steps and with the teacher's self-discipline in the forefront. As he instructed teachers, they are to model the behavior they want in their students. He reminds teachers to address the student behavior, not the actual student. Along the same lines, praise can be dangerous; it should be geared toward student behavior, not the student. Ginott further believed that teachers are at their best when they help pupils develop their self-esteem and to trust their own experiences (Allen, 1996).

The Glasser Model—The Class Meeting

William Glasser wrote a lot about holding class meetings in order to develop discipline on a whole-class starting point (e.g., Glasser 1998a, 1998b, 2000). Rather than teachers imposing discipline over the class, Glasser believed that students are rational and capable of controlling their own behavior if given the chance (Allen, 1996). If the teacher helps the students learn to make good choices, it will produce good behavior. Teachers should not accept excuses for bad behavior, but instead ask the students about the choices they have, why they make certain choices, and how they feel about the results (Allen, 1996).

The Canter Model and the Jones Model—Assertive Discipline

Lee and Marlene Canter and Fred Jones have each worked on assertive discipline models, which are based on observing what successful teachers do (e.g., Canter & Canter, 1992; Jones, 2000). They base their similar theories on several principles, and both models are used in many schools. The Canter Model highlights teachers' rights as educators, as well as student's rights as learners, while the Jones Model highlights incentives, body language, and setting the stage for effective management (Allen, 1996). Assertive discipline basically states that teachers should have firm and consistent control and that their discipline plans should be posted early so that all students know what is expected of them. With assertive discipline, hostile or passive teachers are not effective and their behavior, as such, will only cause confusion and psychological trauma in students (Allen, 1996). This program would replace teacher inertia and hostile behavior with firm, positive insistence, limit setting, and clear expectations. It asserts that lost time can be avoided by systematically employing effective body language, incentive systems, and efficient individual help.

The Skinner Model—Reinforcement of Behavior

B.F. Skinner is commonly known as the father of the behavioral school of psychology. A recently accepted product of Skinnerian behaviorism is known as Behavior Modification, which states that behavior is conditioned by its consequences and strengthened if followed instantly by reinforcement. By this same reasoning, the behavior is weakened if it is not reinforced or if it is punished. Skinner further asserts that behavior can be maintained by irregular reinforcement, such as verbal approval, smiles, and good grades (Allen, 1996).

Creating an Effective Plan

As you have seen, there are a variety of approaches from which to work, and you have had a chance to decide which approach might work best for you. The hopeful outcome is that something presented will work in your classroom with your students and your teaching style. On the other hand, if you read something that you feel will not work for you, save that idea for later and *do not* try it right now.

The main thing is to have a plan with a custom-made fit! But this by itself will not be enough. Even the best plan is useless unless followed consistently. Do not be surprised when the students test the established plan. Essentially, the students will want to test not only the effectiveness of the established plan, but the consistency of the teacher in implementing the plan. Inconsistency leads to the students trying to take advantage of the situation.

Understanding four tenets of human nature will also help you to set up and sustain your plan (Allen, 1996). The first one is that it is human nature for the students to question and resist what others want them to do. Secondly, everyone tends to question authority. Third, it is undeniable that everyone is different with various tastes, likes, abilities, values, and styles. Finally, the last thing is that the teacher is training young people to think for themselves, and part of this process is their tendency to push the limits to see what is valid. All these four things are natural and really quite good in the larger scope of life, as the students work toward learning self-discipline and self-control in their own lives.

As this chapter guides teachers into the process of creating an effective management plan, each teacher can take the chance to critically evaluate the effectiveness of current discipline patterns and the preparation for valuable alterations by answering the questions on pages 209 and 210. Upon critical reflection, the teacher should then be able to analyze the findings and make important decisions toward improving their classroom dynamics in order to improve student behavior.

Things to Look For in Your Own Practice

Question	Your Answer
How effective are your rules, standards, and goals for students?	
What can you do to improve them?	
Have you developed these rules with the students' help?	
Have you given the students time to feel some ownership for them?	
How effective was this process?	
What can you do to increase students' feelings of ownership in your class?	
Have you spent enough time training your students in how you want them to behave?	
How effective was the training?	
What can you do to improve the training of your students?	
Do you present yourself as the best example for the students to follow when you are angry, frustrated, or confused?	

Things to Look For in Your Own Practice *(cont.)*

Question	Your Answer
How effective are you when you are angry, frustrated, or confused?	
What can you do to improve?	
Which student behaviors require attention immediately?	
Which student behaviors can be temporarily ignored?	
Are rules and infractions in your classroom followed by natural consequences?	
List some infractions and consequences that you enforce in your classroom.	
How are they naturally connected?	
What can you do to improve this?	
How effective has your parent communication been?	
What can you do to improve this?	

My Classroom Discipline Plan

You can begin to outline your actual plan on this form. Consider effective rules that you will establish at the onset of the school year and the desired levels of rewards and consequences. Be specific about the considerations surrounding each planned component.

Rules:

1. ______________________
2. ______________________
3. ______________________
4. ______________________
5. ______________________

The incentives for desired behavior:

1. ______________________
2. ______________________
3. ______________________
4. ______________________

Negative consequences in order from the least restrictive to the most restrictive:

1. ______________________
2. ______________________
3. ______________________
4. ______________________

The components of a positive learning environment that will be established:

1. ______________________
2. ______________________
3. ______________________
4. ______________________

Signals that will be used:

1. ______________________
2. ______________________
3. ______________________
4. ______________________

My Classroom Discipline Plan *(cont.)*

Strategies for engaging students during lessons:

1. ______________________________
2. ______________________________
3. ______________________________
4. ______________________________

Important procedures for uninterrupted instructional time (e.g., bathroom breaks, sharpening pencils, drinking water):

1. ______________________________
2. ______________________________
3. ______________________________
4. ______________________________

Plan for communicating with parents:

____
____
____
____

Plan for peer consultation, when needed:

____
____

Plan for documenting management, discipline, and communication problems:

____
____

Plan for the room arrangement:

____
____
____
____
____
____
____

As teachers critically review past teaching practices and then plan for effectively establishing a new system for classroom management and discipline, this chapter has highlighted the importance of guiding students in their academic learning journey. The process begins with a well-established classroom management system. It may be difficult to believe, but most of the time the little and big classroom issues are not specifically related to the teacher, but to all the general issues going on in any student's life. The teacher's job is to train the students for life and to follow through with what is correct and best for student learning. This can be difficult. Research repeatedly shows that the classroom environment directly affects student behavior; this environment includes the physical layout as well as the established routine that intermingles classroom procedures and instructional lessons ("Managing Inappropriate Behavior," 1990). The ultimate goal is to develop self-control in pupils so that they are in control of their own learning progress. That frees the teacher to move away from external, authority-imposed management and allows the teacher to teach and the pupils to learn. This teacher-imposed plan you have just developed can provide for this transition to student self-control and should actually wither away as it is no longer needed. In due course, that is how good discipline should be—self-imposed.

Chapter 10 Reflection

1. What has changed in the way you view your overall management system after reading this book?

2. In what ways have you changed the way you will establish classroom management and discipline practices?

3. Which existing practices have been reinforced after reading the issues presented in this book?

4. What is the correlation between instructional strategies and lesson-delivery methods and classroom management?

References

Allen, T. H. (1996). *Developing a discipline plan for you.* Retrieved October 12, 2006, from http://www.humboldt.edu/~tha1/discip-options.html#results

Behavioral disorders: Focus on change. (1993). Reston, VA: ERIC Clearinghouse on Handicapped and Gifted Children. (ERIC Document Reproduction Service No. ED358674)

Bernshausen, D., & Cunningham, C. (2001, March). *The role of resiliency in teacher preparation and retention.* Paper presented at the 53rd annual meeting of the American Association of Colleges for Teacher Education, Dallas, Texas.

Brooks, J. G., & Brooks, M. G. (1999). *In search of understanding: The case for constructivist classrooms.* Alexandria, VA: Association for Supervision and Curriculum Development.

California Beginning Teacher Support and Assessment. (2006). *BTSA basics.* Retrieved October 4, 2006, from http://www.btsa.ca.gov/BTSA_basics.html

California Teachers Association. (1999). *Behavior contracts.* Retrieved October 20, 2006, from the National Education Association Website: http://www.nea.org/classmanagement/contract.html

Canter, L., & Canter, M. (1992). *Assertive discipline: Positive behavior management for today's classroom* (Rev. ed.). Santa Monica, CA: Canter & Associates.

Carr, J. F., Herman, N., & Harris, D. E. (2005). *Creating dynamic schools through mentoring, coaching, and collaboration.* Alexandria, VA: Association for Supervision and Curriculum Development.

Chelala, C. (2006, January 4). Rich man, poor man: Hungry children in America. *The Seattle Times,* p. B7.

Ciocci, S. R. (2002). *Auditory processing disorders: An overview.* Arlington, VA: ERIC Clearinghouse on Disabilities and Gifted Education. (ERIC Document Reproduction Service No. ED474303)

Clark, A. M. (1999). *Parent-teacher conferences: Suggestions for parents.* Champaign, IL: ERIC Clearinghouse on Elementary and Early Childhood Education. (ERIC Document Reproduction Service No. ED433965)

Clark, R. (2003). *The essential 55.* New York: Hyperion.

Cummins, J. (1991). *Empowering culturally and linguistically diverse students with learning problems.* Reston, VA: ERIC Clearinghouse on Handicapped and Gifted Children. (ERIC Document Reproduction Service No. ED333622)

Darling-Hammond, L. (1998). Teacher learning that supports student learning. *Educational Leadership, 55(5),* 6–11.

Díaz-Rico, L. T., & Weed, K. Z. (2002). *The cross-cultural, language, and academic development handbook: A complete K–12 reference guide* (2nd ed.). Boston: Allyn & Bacon.

Dollase, R. H. (1992). *Voices of beginning teachers.* New York: Teachers College Press.

Doyle, W. (1986). Classroom organization and management. In M. C. Wittrock (Ed.), *Handbook of research on teaching* (3rd ed., pp. 392–431). New York: Macmillan.

Dwyer, K., Osther, D., & Warger, C. (1999). Characteristics of a school that is safe and responsive to all children. *IDRA Newsletter* (May). Retrieved August 26, 2006, from http://www.idra.org/IDRA_Newsletters/May_1999/Characteristics_of_a_School_that_Is_Safe_and_Responsive_to_All_Children/

Eby, J. W., Herrell, A. L., & Jordan, M. L. (2005). *Teaching in K–12 schools: A reflective action approach* (4th ed.). Upper Saddle River, NJ: Prentice Hall.

Echevarria, J., Vogt, M. E., & Short, D. J. (2004). *Making content comprehensible for English language learners: The SIOP model* (2nd ed.). Boston: Allyn & Bacon.

Elam, S. M., Rose, L. C., & Gallup, A. M. (1996). The 28th annual Phi Delta Kappa/Gallup poll of the public's attitudes toward the public schools. *Phi Delta Kappan, 78(1),* 41–59.

Ferraro, J. M. (2000). *Reflective practice and professional development.* Washington, DC: ERIC Clearinghouse on Teaching and Teacher Education. (ERIC Document Reproduction Service No. ED449120)

Fischer, M. (2004). *When students rock the boat, I'm 'master and commander' of my classroom.* Retrieved September 21, 2006, from the Education World Website: http://www.educationworld.com/a_curr/voice/voice127.shtml

Gathercoal, F. (2001). *Judicious discipline* (6th ed.). San Francisco: Caddo Gap Press.

Ginott, H. G. (1993). *Teacher and child: A book for parents and teachers* (Rev. ed). New York: Scribner Paper Fiction.

Ginott, H. G., Ginott, A. (Ed.), & Goddard, H. W. (Ed.). (2003). *Between parent and child* (Rev. ed.). New York: Three Rivers Press.

Girard, K. L. (1995). *Preparing teachers for conflict resolution in the schools.* Washington, DC: ERIC Clearinghouse on Teaching and Teacher Education. (ERIC Document Reproduction Service No. ED387456)

Glasser, W. (1998a). *Choice theory in the classroom* (Rev. ed.). New York: HarperCollins.

Glasser, W. (1998b). *The quality school: Managing students without coercion* (3rd ed.). New York: HarperCollins.

Glasser, W. (2000). *Every student can succeed.* San Diego, CA: Black Forest Press.

Gordon. S. P. (1991). *How to help beginning teachers succeed.* Alexandria, VA: Association for Supervision and Curriculum Development.

Gushee, M. (1984). *Student discipline policies.* Eugene, OR: ERIC Clearinghouse on Educational Management. (ERIC Document Reproduction Service No. ED259455)

Henderson, A. T., & Mapp, K. L. (2002). *A new wave of evidence: The impact of school, family, and community connections on student achievement.* Austin, TX: Southwest Educational Development Laboratory.

Hitz, R., & Driscoll, A. (1989). *Praise in the classroom.* Urbana, IL: ERIC Clearinghouse on Elementary and Early Childhood Education. (ERIC Document Reproduction Service No. ED313108)

Holloway, J. H. (2001). The benefits of mentoring. *Educational Leadership, 58(8),* 85–86.

Hyman, I., Kay, B., Tabori, A., Weber, M., Mahon, M., & Cohen, I. (2006). Bullying: Theory, research, and interventions about student victimization. In C. E. Evertson & C. S. Weinstein (Eds.), *Handbook of classroom management: Research, practice and contemporary issues* (pp. 855–886). Mahway, NJ: Lawrence Erlbaum Associates.

Including students with disabilities in general education classrooms. (1993). Reston, VA: ERIC Clearinghouse on Disabilities and Gifted Education. (ERIC Document Reproduction Service No. ED358677)

Individuals with Disabilities Education Act (IDEA) of 1990, 20 U.S.C. § 1400 *et seq.*

Jones, F. H. (2000). *Tools for teaching.* Santa Cruz, CA: Fredric H. Jones & Associates.

Katz, L. G. (1993). *Self-esteem and narcissim: Implications for practice.* Urbana, IL: ERIC Clearinghouse on Elementary and Early Childhood Education. (ERIC Document Reproduction Service No. ED358973)

Kohn, A. (1994). *The risks of rewards.* Urbana, IL: ERIC Clearinghouse on Elementary and Early Childhood Education. (ERIC Document Reproduction Service No. ED376990)

Kordalewski, J. (1999). *Incorporating student voice into teaching practice.* Washington, DC: ERIC Clearinghouse on Teaching and Teacher Education. (ERIC Document Reproduction Service No. ED440049)

Krashen, S. (1982). *Principles and practice in second language learning and acquisition.* Oxford: Pergamon Press.

Langdon, C. A. (1996). The third Phi Delta Kappan poll of teachers' attitudes toward the public schools. *Phi Delta Kappan, 78(3)*, 244–250.

Lokerson, J. (1992). *Learning disabilities: Glossary of some important terms.* Reston, VA: ERIC Clearinghouse on Handicapped and Gifted Children. (ERIC Document Reproduction Service No. ED352780)

Lumsden, L. (1998). *Teacher morale.* Eugene, OR: ERIC Clearinghouse on Educational Management. (ERIC Document Reproduction Service No. ED422601)

Managing inappropriate behavior in the classroom. (1990). Reston, VA: ERIC Clearinghouse on Handicapped and Gifted Children. (ERIC Document Reproduction Service No. ED371506)

Marshall, M. (2003). Curriculum, instruction, classroom management, and discipline. *Teacher's.net Gazette, 4(2)*. Retrieved September 24, 2006, from http://teachers.net/gazette/FEB03/marshall.html

Marzano, R. J., Marzano, J. S., & Pickering, D. J. (2003). *Classroom management that works: Research-based strategies for every teacher.* Alexandria, VA: Association for Supervision and Curriculum Development.

National Education Association. (1999). *The mentor's 13 jobs: Helping beginning teachers learn to teach.* Retrieved September 17, 2006, from the NEA Website: http://www.nea.org/mentoring/ment030822.html

National Education Association. (2006). *Attracting and keeping quality teachers.* Retrieved September 17, 2006, from the NEA Website: http://www.nea.org/teachershortage/index.html

Nelsen, J., Lott, L., & Glenn, H. S. (2000). *Positive discipline in the classroom* (3rd ed.). New York: Three Rivers Press.

The New Teacher Project. (2006). *Who we are: Overview.* Retrieved October 4, 2006, from http://www.tntp.org/whoweare/overview.html

New York State Education Department. (2006). *Mentoring requirement.* Retrieved October 11, 2006, from http://www.highered.nysed.gov/tcert/faqmentoring.htm

Rose, L. C., & Gallop, A. M. (2003). The 35th annual Phi Delta Kappa/Gallup poll of the public's attitudes toward the public schools. *Phi Delta Kappan, 85(1),* 41–56.

Rose, L. C., & Gallop, A. M. (2004). The 36th annual Phi Delta Kappa/Gallup poll of the public's attitudes toward the public schools. *Phi Delta Kappan, 86(1),* 41–52.

Rowley, J. (1999). The good mentor. *Educational Leadership, 56(8)*, 20–22.

Sanacore, J. (1997). *Student diversity and learning needs.* Bloomington, IN: ERIC Clearinghouse on Reading English and Communication. (ERIC Document Reproduction Service No. ED412527)

Scherer, M. (1998). Perspectives: The importance of being a colleague. *Educational Leadership, 55(5)*, 5.

Starr, L. (2005). *Creating a climate for learning: Effective classroom management techniques.* Retrieved September 21, 2006, from the Education World Website: http://www.education-world.com/a_curr/curr155.shtml

Teaching children with Attention Deficit/Hyperactivity Disorder: Update 1998. (1998). Reston, VA: ERIC Clearinghouse on Disabilities and Gifted Education. (ERIC Document Reproduction Service No. ED423633)

Walz, G. R. (1991). *Counseling to enhance self-esteem.* Ann Arbor, MI: ERIC Clearinghouse on Counseling and Personnel Services. (ERIC Document Reproduction Service No. ED328827)

Wong, H. K., & Wong, R. T. (1998). *How to be an effective teacher: The first days of school.* Mountain View, CA: Harry K. Wong Publications.

Wood, T., & McCarthy, C. (2002). *Understanding and preventing teacher burnout.* Washington, DC: ERIC Clearinghouse on Teaching and Teacher Education. (ERIC Document Reproduction Service No. ED477726)